THE BEST OF

MAURITIAN COOKING

THE BEST OF
MAURITIAN
COOKING

BARRY ANDREWS · PAUL JONES · GERALD GAY

LES·EDITIONS·DU·PACIFIQUE

CONTENTS

La Brigade

Gerald

Michel Rostang

Barry and Paul

Michel Rostang

(1) 47 63 40 77
20 RUE RENNEQUIN, 75017 PARIS
(ANGLE DE LA RUE GUSTAVE-FLAUBERT)
TELEX ROSTANG 649-629 F

Everyone knows the Island of Mauritius - either through personal experience, or as a dream place - the wild landscape of sugar cane, the surrounding sea with its deep and luminous colours and the legendary kindness of the Mauritian people.

In this book, Paul Jones and Barry Andrew introduce you to recipes carefully chosen to be both a pleasure - and a summing up.

A pleasure because they reveal the secrets of great eating, and a summing up of the whole panorama of Mauritius, revealing the tremendous richness and variety of the gastronomical products of the country.

A passion for food can sometimes go too far, but where is any passion without excess?

Here, I should pay tribute to the Island of Mauritius for the multitudinous colours and fragrances which characterize it.

Making a success of these recipes will not require great feats of culinary skill for the reader - all that's needed is attention to detail, and a little patience.

The recipes are in fact Mauritian Cooking without tears and full of the heart and colour of the country.

Do read this book which has such a holiday spirit and recall, fondly, "L'Isle de France".

Michel Rostang

Michel Rostang
Paris, May 1986

Paul Jones.

INTRODUCTION

The pear-shaped island of Mauritius is bathed by the warm cobalt blue waters of the Indian Ocean and fringed by a foamed-washed, coral reef. It lies just north of the Tropic of Capricorn 800 km away from the eastern coast of Madagascar and 200 km from the island of Reunion. The island is 61 km long and 47 km wide, covering a total area of 1865 sq km (around 720 sq m), which is about the same size as the English county of Buckinghamshire or that of Surrey.

Oddly-shaped mountain peaks wind down to gleaming, powder-soft, white beaches constantly washed by the gentle waters of the crystal-clear lagoon, which is forever changing colour, from pale green to turquoise to deep blue.

There is just enough rainfall to keep the island green throughout the year. Sugar cane thrives everywhere. Around the coastal regions, palm and coconut trees compete with the "singing" *filao* or casuarina trees, rightly described as the Mauritius "Aeolian harp". Strong and brilliant colours explode everywhere from exotic plants such as hibiscus, bougainvillia, croton, cassia and oleander.

Though it had been discovered and probably visited by Malays and by Arab sailors from the Gulf (figuring even on one of their *portulans* (charts) of AD 1502), this uninhabited, virgin island remained free from human interference until the 16th century, when the Portuguese captain, Domingo Fernandez, landed in 1511. The Portuguese were later to give the name Mascarenes to the island group of Mauritius, Rodrigues and Réunion, after Pedro Mascarenhas, another Portuguese navigator who also sailed these waters.

The Dutch, however, were the first settlers, naming the island, in 1598, after Prince Maurice of Nassau. Their first landing is recorded in 1558, when Admiral Van Warwijck sailed into the natural harbour of old Grand Port, near Mahébourg, off the south-east coast. The first settlement was not until 80 years later, when a fort was built at what was then called Port South-East. But most of all, the Dutch were

responsible for introducing what later proved to be the mainstay of the economy, sugar-cane, building the first sugar mill on the island.

During the 72 years of their occupation, the Dutch settlers were not happy with conditions in Mauritius. Cyclones, storms and rats are the causes put forward for their departure twice in the period and finally in 1710. The famous international expression "As dead as the Dodo" owes its origin to the Dutch who found, on the island, this unique, ungainly, defenceless bird, called it *Doudo* meaning simpleton, and proceeded to polish it off at huge feasts of barbequed game bird. As if to make up for their sins, the Dutch compensated for this by introducing the spotted deer, imported from Java, which was later to provide sport for the French sugar barons.

For five years after the Dutch had left for good, the island remained uninhabited and wild. It was however, often visited by passing ships and marauding pirates who infested the Indian Ocean, lying in wait for merchantmen trading on the spice route to and from India.

Then, the French, under Captain Guillaume Dufresne Darsel, took possession of Mauritius in 1715 and promptly renamed it *Isle de France*. For the first 30 years, little was done to develop the island, and it was not until a new Governor, François Mahé de Labourdonnais, was appointed in 1745, that things started to get moving. He rebuilt Port Louis, which is still the capital and main port today, and laid down the firm foundations on which the island was to thrive as a prosperous agricultural and commercial centre.

Because Mauritius had become a nest of pirates (especially the deadliest of them all, Surcouf) who endangered the safety of the British East India Company route round the Cape and took heavy toll of their richly-laden ships, the British captured the island in 1810.

With British occupation, the island was renamed Mauritius and remained a colony up to 1968 when Independence was granted, thereby ending 150 years of British rule. That period, during which slavery was also abolished, was very fruitful and in the true spirit of British fair-play, the French language, culture and judicial system were allowed to flourish alongside those of the British.

English is still the official language, although Creole and French, spoken widely in every Mauritius home, office and in official circles, are more commonly heard. The Westminster system of Parliament continues and the Queen is represented by a Governor-General who is now a Mauritian.

Who, then, are those Mauritians who make up the population, which grew from nil to over a million in less than 350 years? Mauritius is often called a "melting pot" due to the diverse ethnic origins of the peoples that came to Mauritius to settle. Those of European descent have dwindled to less than 10,000, most of whom are of French origin. Settlers from India, both Hindu and Muslim, now constitute by far the majority of the population, followed by Creoles of mixed descent and by Chinese.

This impressive cocktail of races, religions, cultures and customs has given rise to a unique population, extremely friendly, with broad flashing smiles and a great willingness to share the best that this nation has to offer with visitors from overseas.

The internationally-known painter, poet and writer, Malcolm de Chazal, once wrote, "*We in Mauritius are a meeting place of many peoples. We are a cross-road; we are an alchemist's retort in which Western and Eastern thoughts meet and combine; we are the crucible of a new civilisation. So we may be a laboratory in which our peoples may be able to set mankind on a new road and to create a new humanism*".

With so many religions practised in Mauritius, there are many very interesting, colourful festivals. *Maha Shivatree* is, without doubt the largest and most dignified in its quiet religious fervour, with thousands of pilgrims making their way slowly to *Grand Bassin* — a natural lake in the centre of the island.

Holi, celebrated in March, is probably the most colourful of Indo-Mauritian festivals. Participants dance and "play" in each other's houses, or outside in official celebrations, throwing brightly coloured water at each other. The result is a feast for the eye and a marvellous opportunity for the amateur or professional photographer.

Tourists visiting Mauritius in October will be fortunate to see the *Divali* festival of light, when homes in villages all over the island are decorated with small candle lights. Symbolically retracing Rama's odyssey, and also commemorating the Hindu God Krishna's destruction of the demon Narakasuran, this festival celebrates the triumph of light over darkness and of virtue over vice.

During December and January, the highly colourful Tamil festival of *Cavadee* includes the equally impressive fire-walking ceremony in which the participants (sometimes even young children and babes in their mothers' arms) have their bodies — including their tongues — pierced by long, sharp needles, metal spikes and hooks!

Nothing symbolizes Mauritian joy and spontaneity more than the *sega* — a dance originally from Africa but since watered down for

indoor shows, only coming into its own when it is danced in some fishing villages at Tamarin and Le Morne, especially. This dance is widely acclaimed as the national dance of the island. One has to understand a little of the history of the island and its people to appreciate the eating habits of Mauritians. The immigrants brought with them their own tastes and preferences, which had to adapt to the various local foodstuffs.

Breakfast follows the Continental habit rather than the English, so that tea or coffee accompanied by bread, toast or croissant is how the majority of Mauritians start the day.

Lunch can be anything from *dholl poori*, an Indian-inspired pancake made of *dholl* (cooked and pureed yellow split peas) filled with spicy chutney, to a slice of fresh pineapple or even *gateau-piment* (chilli-cake rolled in *dholl*). Workers often carry their own lunch in a *tente* (a hold-all basket) containing a metal box in which one finds rice and the accompaniment to the rice — a curry, a *rougaille* (a tomato-based stew) or some salted fish. A *pain maison* (this is actually home-delivered bread but not home-made: so-called because in former days, it was left on the doorstep by hawkers) is also a popular alter-native, filled with anything from a *rougaille* to ham to an *achard* (mustard-seed and fruit pickle) filling. The evening meal generally follows a similar pattern using rice as the main dish, accompanied by one of the many traditional — and delicious — recipes to be found in this book.

What, then, is Mauritius cuisine? Each wave of immigration brought with it cultural and religious influences so the same amalgam of races which make up the population have also created the typical Mauritian cuisine. But on my arrival in Mauritius in 1975 as the Food and Beverage Manager of the first international hotel on the island, I found the delicious local cuisine missing from the menus, replaced by mediocre Continental dishes.

As an Englishman, I had come to Mauritius expecting to find a myriad of fish and seafood dishes, spicy and exotic recipes made up with unusual

tropical ingredients. Instead, there was an abundance of third-grade frozen meat poorly prepared and using packaged spices.

Chef Barry Andrews and I really had to struggle hard to get to the heart and soul of the Mauritian cuisine. It was almost as if people were ashamed of the dishes which the island had produced throughout the years. The older generation were, fortunately, clinging to the past, scorning younger ones who were more interested in westernised food. The recipes were not handed down as before and with the pressures of modern-day living, meal-preparation time had been reduced to a minimum in most Mauritian homes.

But most tourists were also quite determined in their desire to taste local dishes made with different and exotic ingredients. Providing the ingredients was becoming a challenge — overcoming the excess of demand over supply. The farmers and fishermen were having a tough time keeping up with the pace of development of the tourist industry. As a result of great effort, many fruits and vegetables previously not grown on the island have now been successfully introduced, thereby widening the choice of dishes in hotels and restaurants. Various newly-planted herbs and spices are now also extending the wide range of flavours open to chefs and home cooks.

The waves of immigration brought with them the influences of three of the greatest cuisines of the world — French, Indian and Chinese, and of course, the indigenous Creole cuisine.

Creole is a word with many meanings, though, etymologically, the word used to apply only to children born in the colonies from European parents. But today, the most widely-accepted definition is that of a

person of mixed Negro and European descent. Therefore, Mauritian cuisine is a combination of African and European dishes.

Basic ingredients are tomatoes, called in Mauritius "Pommes d'Amour", which provide colour and flavour, onions (when Mauritius runs out of onions, it is said that the stomachs of the nation groan with dismay!) chillies and garlic. Ginger is also a frequent additive, providing another interesting dimension to the food.

Rougaille and *Vindaye* (a composed fish dish with saffron and onions) are among the two most popular preparations of Creole food, both deriving their name from the French word for garlic, "ail" (vindaye is a corruption of the provençal "vin d'ail"). Both are, however, entirely different, the latter being served cold and containing crushed mustard seeds and vinegar rather than tomatoes.

The French, always conservative in their habits, came to Mauritius in galleons laden with traditional French favourites, pâtes, cheeses and wines. However, they quickly discovered that rich, heavy sauces do not go down well in the hot and humid climate and so their cuisine departed from the traditions preached by Saulnier and Escoffier. They started borrowing from other local cuisines, even developing a palate for spicy food, which, they quickly discovered, teases and whets the appetite, (if not the whistle) during the warm, humid days of the Mauritian summer from November to April.

Palm Hearts, camarons (large prawns), wild boar and venison (*cerf*) are firm favourites with today's Franco-Mauritian, the first two being mixed together in a soufflé, to which is added a red sauce made from crushed camaron shells and heads.

Indian cuisine which, without

doubt, constitutes the most important stream of modern-day Mauritian cooking, came with the Indians who started arriving in strength in the early 1800s, especially after the abolition of slavery in 1835. Rice then quickly replaced *manioc* or *cassava* as the staple diet of Mauritians, which it still remains to this day.

Chillies are unquestionably the most commonly-known spice and, fortunately, they either grow wild or are grown in most parts of the island. Tamarind is also frequently used. Grown on trees of the same name, the long green pods turn brown as they ripen revealing a dark sticky brown flesh, which is deliciously bitter. Other spices used are more fully described in Chapter 7 on page 106.

Hindu cuisine is certainly a wonderful marriage of meats (except beef), or fish, or vegetables with exotic spices that tend to emphasise the flavours of the main ingredients rather than overwhelm them.

The night before an Indian wedding ceremony, guests are invited to the parents' house to partake of a traditional meal, comprising seven curries and chutneys served on a banana leaf, together with Indian bread in the form of *pooris* (made from wheat flour) and *dholl poori*, made from yellow split peas. This is, without doubt, one of the most delicious meals I have ever tasted.

Muslim Indians celebrate with a *briani*, which is a delicious mixture of rice, potatoes and spices to which is added chicken, goat, beef or vegetables and all cooked together. Another of my favourites.

The Chinese immigrants from the mainland and Hong Kong succeeded in introducing and gaining widespread acceptance for their own very special cuisine. Chinese cuisine varies greatly in style depending on the region from whence it originates ie. Pekinese, Cantonese or Szechuan. It is probably the latter which is more popular in Mauritius, due to its characteristically highly spiced flavouring.

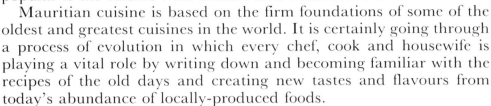

Today there are at least a dozen good restaurants, specialising in very well prepared Chinese food, spread all over the island, so popular is the cuisine with tourists and Mauritians alike.

Mauritian cuisine is based on the firm foundations of some of the oldest and greatest cuisines in the world. It is certainly going through a process of evolution in which every chef, cook and housewife is playing a vital role by writing down and becoming familiar with the recipes of the old days and creating new tastes and flavours from today's abundance of locally-produced foods.

Very few tourists visit the island only once. Many become nostalgic for the island and can't wait to return. Barry and I hope that the recipes in this book will help you overcome, temporarily at least, not only the pangs of hunger but also the yearning to return to our lovely island. For, like its cuisine, Mauritius, once tasted, will dwell in the memory and beckon you back to that island, the motto of which is, "the star and key of the Indian Ocean".

Paul Jones

SAVOURY

AWAKENINGS

Commonly known as snacks or starters, in French, *Hors-d'Oeuvre*, they all perform one important function, and that is to awaken or tease the palate, preparing it for more to come.

They should normally be dainty and tasty, intended to be nibbled away as a delicacy, we are told, and not to be made a meal from.

In Mauritius, snacks are commonly calld *gajaks*, which always accompany drinks before the meal, although tradition has it that the time allocated to drinking is rather more than that reserved for eating. So the *gajaks* are important in the indigenous cuisine and Chinese croquettes, Indian *samoosas*, or *Gateau-Piment*, are the most popular drink-time snacks among the locals.

Our answer to smoked salmon is smoked marlin or sailfish, which is equally delicious. Its popularity is such that the thousands of game fishermen who come from all over the world have a tough time catching enough of them to maintain an adequate supply.

Mauritius, in fact, is one of the finest fishing grounds in the world for the Blue Pacific Marlin and other species of game fish. Until 1982, the World Record for blue marlin was held by Mauritius with a gigantic fish weighing 500 kg, captured off the west coast in 1966.

Black, blue and striped marlin may be caught throughout the year, but especially between October and March. The *La Pirogue Sun "555" Marlin World Cup Competition*, held every year at the beginning of December, attracts entries from all over the world, with demand often far exceeding the inadequate supply of international standard boats.

Often termed "millionaire's salad", heart of palm is without doubt the most sought-after ingredient for our appetizers. Each tree takes three years to reach maturity before being cut down and despatched to kitchens all over the island. Cooked or raw, the palm heart is delicious in both taste and texture and extremely versatile in its ability to combine happily with other foods.

Our oysters (although not as large as the French *Belons* or the English Whitstables) do have a succulent appeal. Found in two varieties, the rock oysters are best raw off the shell with a squeeze of lime, while the larger *huîtres d'argent* lend themselves better to a wide range of cooking, especially with cheese.

Exotic fruits, and the luscious seafood available, combine beautifully in cocktails and salads, providing the chef with a wide range of options and colour combinations for unusual dishes.

CRISPY FRIED PRAWNS

500 gm shelled large prawns
15 gm cornflour; diluted
with a little water
½ egg white
¼ tsp salt
¼ tsp monosodium glutamate (optional)
1 litre vegetable oil
1 chopped spring onion
5 gm chopped, peeled root ginger
1 glass rice wine
15 gm brown sugar
125 ml chicken stock
¼ medium cucumber
cut in half and sliced
2 large Chinese black mushrooms soaked,
drained and sliced
touch of hot chilli sauce

4 servings

Clean the prawns; devein and wash well. Mix the diluted cornstarch, egg white, salt, M.S.G. together. Place the prawns in the above mixture and coat evenly.

Heat oil until very hot. Place the prawns into the oil and fry both sides. When prawns float, remove and drain.

In another pan heat a little oil until quite hot and add the rest of the ingredients, including the leftover batter. Pour in carefully to avoid splattering. Stir all the time until batter is cooked.

Serve|the prawns with Cantonese rice.

Preparation : 15 min • Cooking : 5 min
★ Easy   ☆ Expensive

GINGER FRIED PRAWN BALLS

250 gm minced prawns
60 gm minced pork
3 large minced water chestnuts
1 egg white
pinch salt
1 tblsp sesame oil
1 tblsp rice wine
6 minced spring onions
20 gm minced peeled root ginger
30 gm cornflour
50 gm white bread crumbs
5 gm crushed black peppercorns
500 ml cooking oil
20 gm onion salt

4 servings

Mix together the prawns, pork and water chestnuts with 2 tablespoons of water, mix well to combine.

Gradually stir in the egg white, do not beat. Add the salt, sesame oil, rice wine, spring onion, ginger and cornflour, stir until all the ingredients are blended together.

Form the above mixture into bite-sized balls. Roll these balls into the bread-crumbs and pepper.

Heat oil. When moderately hot, cook the balls in the oil turning over all the time. Cook for approx. 3 minutes.

Remove from the oil and drain. Season with the onion salt just before serving.

Preparation : 20 min • Cooking : 30 min
★ Easy   ☆ Moderate

Previous page: Gâteau Rouille, Samoosa, Gâteau Piment, Allu Purri (p. 35, 23, 31)

GARLIC OYSTERS WITH WHITE WINE

36 oysters
seasoning
120 ml white wine
280 gm white breadcrumbs
2 lemons squeezed for juice
3 cloves garlic, crushed
250 gm unsalted butter
lemon wedges

6 servings

Open the oysters, scrub very well, clean by removing the beards, place on a tray and season. Sprinkle over the white wine.

Place under a hot grill for 3 minutes and then remove.

Mix the remaining ingredients into a paste. Cover the oysters with the garlic butter paste.

Place under the grill until the breadcrumbs are golden brown.

Serve immediately with the lemon wedges.

Note: This recipe can be very easily adapted and made more economical in many countries by using mussels.

After cleaning the mussels well, poach them gently in water or in a court bouillon for around 3 minutes, then proceed as explained above.

Preparation : 10 min • Cooking : 5 min
★ Easy ☆ Expensive

DEEP FRIED OYSTERS ON BROCHETTES

36 fresh oysters
50 ml rice wine
10 gm sliced root ginger
1 spring onion
5 gm salt
30 gm flour
100 gm cornflour
1 lightly beaten egg
200 gm white bread crumbs
10 gm chopped parsley
oil for deep frying

6 servings

Carefully rinse the oysters under cold water and allow to drain.

Mix together the wine, ginger and the chopped spring onion. Marinate the oysters in the above mixture for 20 minutes.

Mix the salt and the flour together. Sieve the cornflour to make it light.

Remove the oysters from the marinade and roll in the cornflour. Spear the oysters onto 12 skewers.

Coat the oysters with the cornflour, then dip into the beaten egg and roll into the white breadcrumbs and parsley. Shake off any excess breadcrumbs.

Heat the oil ready for deep frying and deep fry the brochettes for about 2 minutes. Remove and drain.

Serve with Garlic Sauce.

Preparation : 30 min • Cooking : 2 min
★ Easy ☆ Expensive

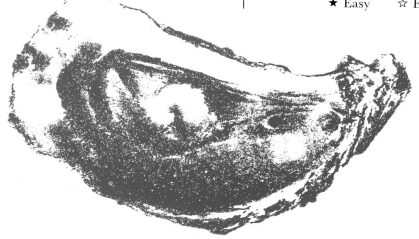

FISH TARTARE

350 gm fillet of white tuna
or any fatty white fish
8 fresh basil leaves very finely chopped
10 gm fresh chervil leaves
very finely chopped
60 ml olive oil
1 large lemon squeezed for the juice
salt and ground pepper

4 servings

Remove any bones or sinews from the fillet of fish.

Chop the fish very finely or process in the blender. Add the chopped herbs, salt and pepper and mix in well.

Whisk the olive oil and lemon together. Add to the fish and mix together. Season to taste.

Spoon out of the bowl into quennelle shapes onto a plate and serve chilled with melba toast.

Melba toast: grill slices of bread either side, cut the toast horizontally along the middle of the two toasted sides.

Scrape off any surplus soft bread and cut in half.

Replace under a grill on a low heat to dry out.

Melba toast can also be made in the oven. After toasting and cutting it in half as explained above, place in slow oven 100°F (40°C) and leave until completely dried out.

Best served fresh or you can store the toast in an airtight tin for a few days, crisping in the oven before serving.

Preparation : 20 min
★ Easy   ☆ Cheap

RAVIOLI OF SMOKED MARLIN

30 gm cooked white tuna
(or any firm white fish)
125 gm smoked marlin trimmings
or smoked salmon
120 ml double cream
16 slices smoked marlin
or smoked salmon
(approx. 300 gm)
salt

4 servings

Blend together the tuna and the marlin trimmings.

Process in a blender for about 1 minute.

Pass the mixture through a fine sieve into a small bowl.

Place the bowl onto a bed of crushed ice.

Gradually stir in the cream, a little at a time, using a wooden spoon.

Season to taste with the salt.

Lay 8 slices of smoked marlin on a working surface. Divide the creamed fish between the 8 slices in a pile in the centre of the slice.

Place the remaining slices over the top.

Press down a little and cut to desired shape, square or round.

Take a smaller cutter and just press around the edges of the hump to form the ravioli.

Preparation : 20 min
★ Easy   ☆ Expensive

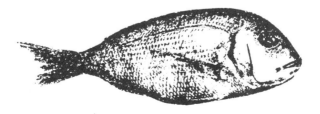

Left: Fish Tartare & Ravioli of Smoked Marlin

FISH ROE SAUTEED IN GARLIC

30 gm plain flour
1 × 120 gm fresh fish roe
60 gm unsalted butter
1 clove crushed garlic
1 pinch salt

2 servings

Sieve together the flour and salt. Heat the butter and garlic in a pan over a low heat. Roll the fish roe into the flour so that it is completely covered.

Place the fish roe into the pan of melted butter. Cook gently for 5 minutes turning over all the time. Remove from the pan when cooked.

Cut into thin slices and serve with rice with chopped coriander and Black Lentils.

This can also be served in Creole Sauce. Heat 250 gm of Creole Sauce and add the cooked fish roe.

Alternatively, the fish roe is simply delicious served by itself with plenty of freshly squeezed lemon juice. Serve heaped on a bed of lettuce.

Preparation : 5 min • Cooking : 5 min
★ Very easy   ☆ Cheap

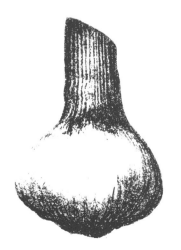

HARE PATE

500 gm pork fat
500 gm hare meat
30 gm unsalted butter
100 gm chicken liver
9 gm salt
1 gm ground black pepper
1 gm five spice powder
½ glass dry red wine
1 tot rum
60 ml fresh cream
75 chopped walnuts
200 gm pistachio nuts
1 egg

10 servings

Line the mould with the pork fat cut into very thin slices. Remove the hare from the bones.

Make a good stock with the bones; reduce the liquid by half and allow to cool. Cook the chicken livers lightly in butter.

Marinate all the meats for 12 hours in the cold stock, salt, pepper, spices, wine and the rum.

Place the marinated meat into the blender with the eggs, fresh cream and a little marinade mixture.

Mix well until smooth. Add the chopped walnuts and pistachio nuts to the mixture.

Place into the pre-prepared mould. Cook in a *"bain marie"* at 180°F (100°C).

When cooked remove from the oven. Pour some hare stock on top of the pâté.

Place into the refrigerator for 4 hours before serving.

Note: Any game meat may be used in the place of the hare.

If the meat is considered too strong in taste it can be soaked in milk overnight. This will remove the gamey taste.

Preparation : 20 min • Cooking : 10 min
★ Difficult   ☆ Expensive

SAMOOSA

280 gm minced beef
45 gm ghee
1 minced onion
2 cloves minced garlic
10 gm minced ginger root
5 gm finely chopped coriander leaves
5 gm turmeric
5 gm mustard seeds
3 minced chillies
20 gm curry powder
juice of one lemon
seasoning
oil for frying

6 servings

For the wrappers of the samoosa use the spring roll recipe (see page 30). Cook the beef in a very little water until the water has evaporated and the meat is dry.

Heat the ghee in a pan. Fry the onion and garlic in the ghee. Do not allow to colour. Add the ginger and the cooked meat to the onion mix. Cook for two minutes.

Add the remaining ingredients and heat thoroughly, stirring with a wooden spoon all the time.

Roll out the pastry to paper thin thickness.

Place the circles on to a heated *tawa* or heavy frying pan. Heat both sides of the pastry for 10 seconds.

Remove and place onto a floured board. Cut each circle into triangles. Fold 2 ends over to form a triangular pocket.

Fill the pocket with the samoosa mixture. Fold the corner over to get a triangular shape. Stick edges down with a little cold water.

Deep fry the samoosa until a golden brown.

Serve hot with mint or peanut chutney.

Preparation : 25 min • Cooking : 3 min
★ Difficult   ☆ Cheap

PIGS' EARS

4 cleaned pigs' ears
6 cloves garlic
60 ml oil
seasoning
milk
1 cinammon stick
4 cloves
30 ml soya sauce
60 gm honey

4 servings

When ordering the ears ask for the flesh around the ears to be left on.

Cut the cloves of garlic lengthways into a 4 pieces each.

Pierce the skin of the ears and place the pieces of garlic and a clove under the skin of each ear.

Heat 45 ml of the oil in a pan. Place the ears in the oil and colour for just a few minutes.

Season to taste.

Pour the milk into the same pan, to cover the ears, with the cinammon stick and the cloves.

Bring to the boil, cover the pan with a lid and allow to simmer until the ears are cooked. When cooked, remove from the liquid and cut into slices.

In another pan, heat the rest of the oil. Add the sliced ears and fry for one minute, turning all the time. Pour on the soya sauce and honey.

Continue to cook gently, allowing the honey to just caramelise.

Turn the ears all the time.

When crispy serve with a Garlic Sauce with a little hot chilli sauce added.

Preparation : 15 min • Cooking : 30 min
★ Difficult   ☆ Cheap

PRAWN AND SESAME SNACK

250 gm peeled prawns
1 lemon squeezed for the juice
1 drop hot chilli sauce
10 gm fresh chervil, finely chopped
10 gm salt
4 slices of bread
30 gm sesame seeds
oil for deep frying

4 servings

Crush the prawns, lemon, chilli sauce and chervil together and blend into a paste, season with the salt.

Spread onto the slices of bread.

Sprinkle the surface of the paste very well with the sesame seeds.

Cut into strips or various shapes and refrigerate for 1 hour.

Heat the oil and deep fry the prawn strips until a golden brown.

This is a delicious snack with drinks, or it can be served as a light lunch with Creole Rice or rice spiced with finely chopped coriander.

Drain and serve immediately.

Preparation : 15 min • Cooking : 5 min
★ Easy   ☆ Moderate

OYSTERS WITH CREOLE SAUCE AND BEARNAISE

36 oysters
seasoning
1 glass white wine
240 gm Creole Sauce
80 gm Bearnaise Sauce

6 servings

Open the oysters, clean by removing the beards, place on a tray and season. Sprinkle white wine over liberally, sufficient to cover them.

Cook in a moderate oven for two minutes.

Remove from oven.

Heat the Creole Sauce and spoon over the oysters.

Spoon over the Bearnaise.

Place under the grill for 2 minutes to brown.

Serve immediately.

Note: This recipe can also be adapted using mussels.

After scrubbing and cleaning the mussels well, poach for a few minutes in water or a court bouillon, then add the sauces and place under the grill.

Preparation : 10 min • Cooking : 5 min
★ Easy   ☆ Expensive

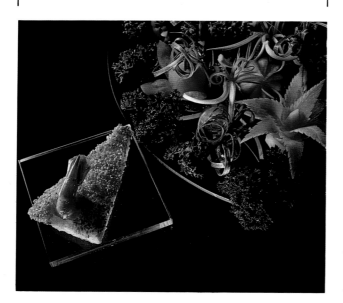

Left: Prawn and Sesame Snack
Top left: Oysters with Creole Sauce and Bearnaise
Top right: Heart of Palm with Lemon (p. 26)
Bottom right: Crayfish Salad (p. 26)

CRAYFISH SALAD

½ kg boiled crayfish
½ small cleaned onion, very thinly sliced
1 small cleaned fresh chilli,
finely chopped
2 medium chopped tomatoes
35 ml olive oil
15 ml malt vinegar
1 lemon squeezed for juice
1 spring onion, finely chopped
cleaned lettuce

2 servings

Remove the crayfish from the shell and cut into slices. Add all the ingredients together and marinate for 2 hours.

Serve on a bed of lettuce leaves.

Garnish with lemon segments, black olive slices and tomato quarters.

Preparation : 20 min
★ Very easy ☆ Expensive

HEART OF PALM WITH LEMON

1 heart of palm (fresh if possible)
3 lemons squeezed for the juice
salt

4 servings

One must work fairly fast once the palm heart has been cut. Remove the outer bark from the heart. Cut this into pieces and cut a U-shape along the edges for decoration if desired. Rub the cut edges with some lemon juice to prevent browning. Cut the heart of palm into a very fine julienne.

Pour over the lemon juice, add salt to taste. Place with palm heart into the four pieces of bark. Decorate with tomato roses, lemon slices and black olives.

Serve immediately.

Preparation : 20 min
★ Easy ☆ Moderate

CHINESE CHICKEN WINGLETS

12 chicken winglets
300 gm raw peeled prawns
30 gm pork fat
1 sprig fresh thyme
30 ml white rum
1 egg white
10 ml sesame oil
10 gm monosodium glutamate (optional)
60 gm cornflour
120 gm crushed roasted peanuts
oil for frying

6 servings

Remove wingtips, then remove large central bone from each of the chicken winglets, slit the meat, flatten it just a little. Then, scrape it down so that all the meat is at the end of the bone. Sprinkle over the winglets 30 gm of the cornflour.

Chop the prawns finely with the pork fat. Chop the thyme very finely.

Mix together the prawns, pork, thyme, rum, egg, sesame oil, seasoning and 30 gm of cornflour. Mix all of these well to form a paste.

Divide the paste into twelve and spread it onto each flattened winglet. Sprinkle the crushed peanuts on top and press into the paste lightly.

Heat the oil for deep frying. Cook the winglets for 3 minutes in the oil until a golden brown.

Remove from the oil, drain and serve immediately.

Preparation : 25 min • Cooking : 3 min
★ Easy ☆ Moderate

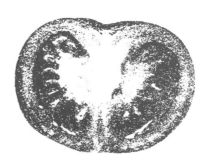

QUAIL SALAD WITH RASPBERRY VINEGAR

1 cleaned lettuce
8 leaves cleaned red cabbage
4 fresh quail
4 quail eggs
50 gm unsalted butter
½ clove crushed garlic
250 gm fresh mushrooms (cleaned)
20 ml raspberry vinegar
50 gm pine nuts

4 servings

Place the lettuce and red cabbage onto the plates. Put the plates into the refrigerator.

Pre-heat the oven to moderate.

Clean the quail and season.

Wrap in silver foil and cook for around 6 minutes.

Remove the bird from the foil and cut along the back.

Open the quail to lay flat and carefully remove the bones.

Set aside and keep warm.

Boil the quail eggs for two minutes, then remove the shell.

Heat 30 gm of the butter in a pan. Cook the garlic and mushrooms gently, do not overcook. Add the raspberry vinegar and toss the mushrooms in the mixture.

Remove from the heat.

Heat the remaining butter in a pan and brown the pine nuts.

Remove the plates from the refrigerator. Place the warm quail, mushrooms, and pine nuts to top of the lettuce.

Spoon over the quail the sauce from the mushrooms.

Serve immediately.

Preparation : 25 min • Cooking : 25 min
★ Easy   ☆ Moderate

DEEP FRIED QUAIL EGG PACKETS

12 fresh quail eggs
2 sheets bean curd or won ton wrappers
1 large egg
90 gm cornflour
15 ml soya sauce
oil for deep frying

6 servings

Boil the quail eggs for 3 minutes. Remove from the water and run under cold water for 3 minutes. This prevents a black rim from forming around the yolk. When the egg is cold carefully remove the shell.

Take the bean curd wrappers and cut into twelve, large enough to wrap the eggs in. Beat the large egg and the cornflour together with the soya sauce. Spread this paste evenly over the bean curd wrappers.

Wrap each egg until it is completely covered. Place in the refrigerator for 5 minutes.

Heat the oil for deep frying. Deep fry the eggs for 2 minutes until a golden brown.

Delicious served with drinks.

Serve immediately.

Preparation : 25 min • Cooking : 2 min
★ Easy   ☆ Cheap

HEART OF PALM CAROLINE

½ litre milk
1 fresh (or canned) heart of palm
250 gm lobster tail (cooked)
200 ml sauce blanche
120 gm cheddar cheese
50 ml fresh cream
60 gm unsalted butter
30 gm parmesan cheese
seasoning

4 servings

Remove the outer bark of the palm heart. Place the tender heart into the milk. Cook gently for about 10 minutes.

Remove from the milk and allow to drain. Cut the bark into 5 individual pieces.

Remove the lobster tail from the shell. Cut into 12 pieces, and keep warm.

Heat the sauce blanche, adding 50 gm. of cheddar cheese. Season. Add the cream and butter and blend at top speed.

Cut the palm heart into 12 rondels. Place the palm heart and lobster pieces alternately in the palm bark pieces. Cover with the Sauce Blanche.

Sprinkle over the remaining cheeses that have been mixed together.

Place under the grill. Serve immediately.

Preparation : 35 min • Cooking : 15 min
★ Easy ☆ Expensive

28

SMOKED MARLIN WITH CAMARON MOUSSE

200 gm fresh camarons
(fresh prawns or lobster may be used)
60 gm smoked marlin or salmon
trimmings
1 egg white
20 gm gelatine, soaked in a little
warm water
360 ml well chilled double cream
12 slices smoked marlin
or smoked salmon
1/2 tsp fine salt

6 servings

Poach the camarons in a court bouillon for about 4 minutes. Scoop out of the boiling bouillon and allow to drain. Remove the flesh from the shells of the camarons. Cut along the back and remove the black vein.

Put the camaron and the smoked marlin pieces into the blender with the egg white. Blend for 1 minute. Rub the puree through a fine sieve. Sieve into a bowl placed on crushed ice.

Dissolve the gelatine on a very low heat.

Gently stir the cream into the fish puree with a wooden spoon. Pour in a little cream at a time, stirring gently but continuously. Add the salt.

Pour in the liquid gelatine stirring all the time.

Lay the 12 slices of smoked marlin on a work surface.

Divide the mousse between the slices. Roll up each slice to form a neat roll. Place on a rack and into the refrigerator.

Serve with lemon or a creamy horseradish sauce.

Preparation : 25 min
★ Difficult   ☆ Expensive

Top: Heart of Palm Caroline
Bottom: Smoked Marlin with Camaron Mousse

SPRING ROLLS

Wrappers:

250 gm plain flour
15 gm salt
90 ml warm water
15 ml olive oil

Sieve the flour and salt together. Add the water and the oil to the salt and flour and form a smooth paste. Place on a floured board and knead gently for 5 minutes. The paste will become elastic and easier to roll.

When kneading is completed, cover with a damp cloth, allow to stand in a warm place for a good 10 minutes.

Take a piece of dough and place on a floured board. With a floured rolling pin press down on the paste as hard as possible and roll hard. This makes the pastry thin and transparent which is essential.

Take care not to break the pastry: it is very fragile at this stage.

Cut into squares 15 cm across and cover with a damp cloth. Proceed with the remaining dough as above.

When completed cut the squares into two triangular shaped pieces.

Preparation : 25 min
★ Difficult   ☆ Cheap

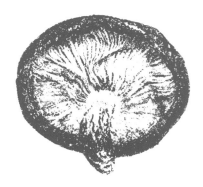

Filling:

8 fresh coriander leaves
6 chopped water chestnuts
4 minced spring onions
8 large, soaked Chinese mushrooms
100 gm lightly fried minced pork
1 large grated carrot
50 gm bean sprouts
50 gm chopped cooked prawns
20 gm cornflour
5 gm salt
1½ tsp dark soya sauce
10 gm white sugar
2 cloves crushed garlic
1 crepin of pig (optional)
oil for frying

4 servings

Finely chop the coriander leaves. Soak the Chinese mushrooms in water for 20 minutes. Drain and cut into shreds. Place all of the ingredients together except the crepin of pig. Mix well in a bowl.

Place the oil in a pan and heat on a fast heat.

Put all the ingredients into the pan and cook for one minute. Stir fry to prevent burning. Allow to cool.

Place a heaped tablespoon of filling on a square piece of crepin. Turn in the two ends and fold over the crepin to form a roll. If not using crepin, place filling directly onto pastry.

Place the rolled filling onto the triangular pastry. Turn in the two ends and fold over to form a roll. Stick the last piece of pastry down with water.

When completed, refrigerate for half an hour, allowing to stand.

Heat oil for deep frying, and dip spring rolls into the oil. Fry until golden brown and drain.

Before serving return to the hot oil for half a minute to crispen.

Serve with soya sauce.

The spring roll can also be dipped into beaten egg on the second frying.

Preparation : 20 min • Cooking : 5 min
★ Difficult   ☆ Moderate

ALLU PURRI

1 kilo cleaned and boiled potatoes
250 gm cooked minced beef
1 small cleaned chilli
10 gm salt
12 leaves fresh coriander finely chopped
10 gm finely chopped parsley
3 black peppercorns finely crushed
2 cloves crushed garlic
10 gm crushed root ginger
1 sprig fresh thyme
5 gm caraway powder
10 ml vegetable oil
60 gm plain flour
2 large eggs
oil for deep frying

6 servings

Cream the boiled potatoes with 1 pinch salt. When smooth put aside and keep warm.

Ensure that after cooking the minced beef is quite dry. Crush the chilli with a little salt.

Mix together the meat, chilli, coriander, parsley, pepper, garlic, ginger, thyme, caraway and the 10 ml of oil. Season to taste.

Make a ball of the creamed potatoes, weighing approximtely 50 gm. Place the ball in one hand and press a hole in the potato.

Fill the hole with the meat mixture and press over the potato to cover the mixture. You will have a ball of potato filled with meat. Continue in this way until the mixture and the potato is finished.

Beat the eggs with a little salt. Heat the oil until quite hot. Roll the potato balls in the flour.

Dip into the egg, drain well and then place into the deep frying oil. Fry until a golden brown.

Remove from the oil, drain and serve hot with tamarind chutney.

Preparation : 30 min • Cooking : 5 min
★ Easy   ☆ Moderate

GATEAU PIMENT WITH CORIANDER

½ kilo dholl (yellow split peas)
10 gm anis (cummin) or soja
2 medium, cleaned and finely chopped chillies
4 spring onions
1 pinch salt
1 pinch saffron powder
1 large egg
1 sprig freshly chopped coriander leaves
oil for frying

4 servings

Wash and clean the dholl thoroughly. Put the dholl into 125 ml of water and boil for 5 minutes. Strain well and place on a cloth to dry.

Crush the anis or, if using soja, chop finely. Put the dholl onto a *roche carri* and crush, or use a blender.

Add all the ingredients to the crushed dholl. Mix in thoroughly with a wooden spoon.

Heat the oil in a pan until very hot.

Make small balls with the paste and drop them into the oil carefully. Fry until crisp and golden brown outside.

Remove from the pan, drain and eat while hot and crisp.

Preparation : 35 min • Cooking : 20 min
★ Easy   ☆ Cheap

TROPICAL ISLAND COCKTAIL IN COCONUT

250 gm cocktail sauce
1 drop tabasco
1 orange zest and juice
1 tot brandy
90 gm whipped cream
18 camarons
3 yellow coconuts
1 fresh palm heart
2 lemons squeezed for juice
3 boiled eggs
lettuce

6 servings

To the cocktail sauce, add the tabasco, orange zest, juice, brandy and whipped-cream.

Boil some court bouillon and cook the fresh camarons for 8 minutes.

Remove the cooked camarons from the court bouillon and allow to cool.

Peel and clean 12 of the camaron and cut each into four pieces. Cut the yellow coconuts in half. Keep the coconut water. Chill and drink!

Clean and dry the lettuce. Cut into a fine julienne.

Take the heart of palm and peel off the hard bark. Cut the tender part of the heart into fine pieces.

Pour the lemon juice over the palm heart to prevent it from going brown.

Cut the whites of the boiled eggs into a fine julienne. Add to the palm heart.

Fold in half of the cocktail sauce. Take the lettuce and line each of the coconuts with them.

Divide the palm heart mixture and place on top of the lettuce. Spoon over the remainder of the cocktail sauce.

Decorate with a camaron on top and serve immediately.

Preparation : 30 min • Cooking : 5 min
★ Difficult   ☆ Expensive

Right: Tropical Island Cocktail in Coconut
Far right: Avocado Butterfly with Seafood Annette.

AVOCADO MOUSSE WITH NUTMEG

2 large mashed avocados
juice of 1 lemon
seasoning
1 pinch ground nutmeg
1 finely chopped spring onion
½ cup mayonnaise
¼ cup hot water
1 tsp gelatine powder
1 cup cream

4 servings

Place the mashed avocados in a bowl.

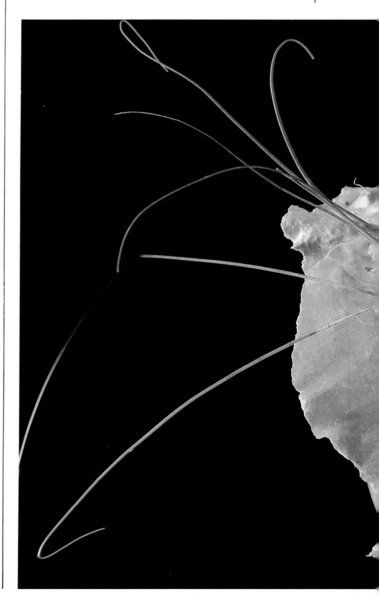

Add the lemon juice, salt, pepper, nutmeg and spring onion. Fold the mayonnaise into the above mixture.

Put the hot water into a cup and sprinkle the gelatine on top. Stir until dissolved and allow to cool.

Whisk the cream until thick. Fold the cool gelatine into the avocado mix. Fold in the whipped cream.

Spoon the mousse into a mould and chill for four hours. When ready, turn out onto a platter.

To facilitate turning out, place the mould in hot water for 30 seconds.

Preparation : 20 min
★ Very easy   ☆ Moderate

AVOCADO BUTTERFLY WITH SEAFOOD ANNETTE

120 gm cleaned boiled prawns
90 gm peeled cucumber, finely diced
90 gm cleaned pineapple, finely diced
¼ tsp cleaned root ginger, finely grated
500 gm boiled langouste out of the shell
50 ml fresh whipped cream
1 orange, finely grated for the zest
1 tot brandy
120 gm cocktail sauce
2 large peeled avocado
paprika and black olives

Mix the prawns, cucumber, pineapple and root ginger. Slice the langouste in 12.

Fold the cream, orange zest, brandy and cocktail sauce together gently. Mix 60 gm of this mixture with the prawns.

Cut the avocado pears in four. Cut each quarter into a fan from the thick end (this is the wings of the butterfly.) Place two wings on plates and spoon the prawn mixture in the centre (for the body).

Place three slices of langouste on top of this mixture. Cover over with the remaining cocktail sauce. Decorate with paprika and the olives.

Preparation : 15 min
★ Difficult   ☆ Expensive

AVOCAT BELLE MARE

4 rondels palm heart
80 gm white crab meat
30 gm unsalted butter
2 dsrtsp Red Sauce
1 tot brandy
1 medium avocado pear
30 gm grated cheddar cheese
seasoning

2 servings

Cook the rondels of palm heart in hot milk until tender. Take the white meat from the crab and flake it.

Melt the butter in a pan. Add the crab meat to the butter and cook gently. Season to taste. Add enough Red Sauce just to bind the crab meat together. Add the brandy.

Place the cooked palm heart on to a serving dish. Peel and cut the avocado pear in half, remove the stone. Cut the halves in half again lengthways. Turn the avocado pieces so that each piece is back to back. Put these pieces on to the palm heart roundels.

Place the crab meat in the middle of the pieces of avocado. Cover only the crab meat with a little more heated Red Sauce.

Sprinkle the Red Sauce with the grated cheese.

Brown the cheese under a very hot grill for one minute. Serve immediately.

Preparation : 20 min • Cooking : 15
★ Easy   ☆ Expensive

PALM HEART CREOLE STYLE

12 large fresh camarons
or fresh prawns in the shell
1 fresh palm heart (or canned)
3 cups creole sauce page
milk

6 servings

Poach the camarons in a court bouillon.

Cook the palm heart in sufficient milk to cover. When the palm heart is soft but firm, remove from the milk and cut into julienne.

Cut the harder part of the palm bark into portion size pieces (This is the outer shell that cannot be eaten).

They will be used later for serving.

If using canned palm heart, drain, cut into julienne and proceed with recipe.

Heat the Creole Sauce and fold the palm heart into it. Place the Creole Sauce and palm heart mixture into this shell.

Split the tails of the camarons into two, up to the heads only. Remove the black veins in their tails.

The camaron heads should then stand upright on the split tails. Place on either side of the palm shells.

Garnish with parsley, spring onion and lemon wedges. Serve hot.

Preparation : 15 min • Cooking : 15 min
★ Easy   ☆ Expensive

GATEAU ROUILLE

*120 gm rouille cleaned and coarsely
grated
30 gm cornflour
5 gm crushed root ginger
3 gm salt
water
oil for deep frying*

12 pieces

Mix the rouille, cornflour and ginger together. Add the salt. Add a little water and mix together.

One must be able to form a ball and maintain the shape.

Heat the oil to a medium heat.

Place the gateaux into the oil. Fry until a golden brown, scoop out of the oil. Allow to drain and serve hot.

In place of the rouille one can also use white cabbage, finely chopped.

Note: There are two types of rouille, one is white, the other violet. For this recipe use the violet type.

One may also boil the rouille whole, then slice and eat hot with butter. It can also be grated, mixed with chopped onions and made into 'hash browns'.

If cleaned, cut into chips and deep fried it is very tasty.

The Chinese often boil the rouille, puree the cooked flesh, mix with corn stock, roll into a small ball and dip the ball into a beaten egg. It is then fried to a golden brown.

Preparation : 10 min • Cooking : 5 min
★ Very easy ☆ Cheap

STUFFED CHILLIES

*16 large green chillies
½ medium onion finely chopped
500 gm minced beef
1 sprig fresh thyme, finely chopped
½ clove crushed garlic
seasoning
30 gm plain flour
½ tsp baking powder
½ tsp turmeric
oil for deep frying
water
salt*

4 servings

Cut the top (stalk end) off of the end of the chilli. With a small knife remove the seeds without breaking the chilli. Wash under running cold water to remove any surplus seeds and dry.

Heat a little oil in the pan. Cook the onions but do not allow to colour. Add the minced beef and stir with a wooden spoon. Add the thyme and garlic and cook for five minutes. Season to taste.

When the meat is cooked, strain off any surplus liquid. Make a smooth batter beating well the flour; baking powder, turmeric and water. Season. Pass through a fine strainer.

Stuff the chillies with the beef mixture.

Heat enough oil for deep frying. Dip the stuffed chillies into the batter, and drain off excess batter. Drop gently into the hot oil. Cook until golden brown.

Serve immediately.

Preparation : 10 min • Cooking : 10 min
★ Easy ☆ Cheap

THE
MELTING POT

In every country, soups have pride of place in the everyday cuisine. Very often constituting a meal in themselves, soups are both economical and can be most nutritious.

A good soup is only as good as the ingredients that go into its making and therefore, bearing that in mind, one has to take care to use only the best and freshest ingredients, not, as is often the case, "leftovers". One should also remember the following credo in serving soups; cold soups must be served icy-cold in chilled soup cups and hot soups, piping hot, in pre-heated cups or bowls.

Grimod de la Reyniere described soups beautifully when he said: "It is to a dinner what a portico or a peristyle is to a building; that is to say, it is not only the first part of it, but it must be devised in such a manner as to set the tone of the whole banquet, in the same way as the overture of an opera announces the subject of the work".

Modern-day household aids, such as the liquidizer found in most homes, have contributed towards the invention of many soups and sauces. The ease with which one can turn almost anything into a puree has made many housewives keen to experiment and they have produced, at times, quite spectacular results.

Sauces are the supreme test of the master chef. They demand great care and attention, using only the finest ingredients for the base. As one proceeds through the method of preparation, one has to taste constantly to correct and "tune" the flavour balance and seasoning. Probably the most versatile and often-used sauce in Mauritius is the Creole sauce, which is served as a piquant accompaniment to most meats, fish, seafood and vegetables.

Both soups and sauces require a good base which is generally called stock. You can make stock from beef, veal, fish bones or poultry carcasses, depending on the specific flavouring required.

That the melting pot of Mauritius has contributed in no small degree to international cuisine cannot be denied, and this might well have been in the mind of the famous 19th century philosopher Brillat-Savarin when he wrote, "And you gastronomes of 1825, already sated in the midst of plenty, and dreaming now of dishes, you will never know the mysteries science shall reveal in 1900.

"You will never see what travellers as yet unborn shall bring from that half of the globe which still remains to be discovered or explored. *How I Pity You.*"

WATERCRESS BOUILLON

200 gm watercress leaves
oil for frying
1 large onion, finely chopped
3 cloves crushed garlic
5 gm root ginger, finely grated
750 ml water
1 drop Hot Chilli Sauce
seasoning

6 servings

Use only the watercress on a thin stem.

Heat a very little oil in a pan. Fry the onion until soft but not brown. Add the crushed garlic and ginger. Mix together with a wooden spoon. Add the water to the pan. Bring to the boil, and add the Hot Chilli Sauce.

Add the watercress leaves and remove the pan from the fire, season to taste. Serve immediately.

Note: The watercress must be served green. If boiled or left too long in the water the leaves will turn brown.

This dish may be used in many ways. As a soup, on its own, or served as an accompaniment with rice.

At home, the stock from boiled rice is sometimes used in place of water.

Other local greens that can be used are: *brede mouron, brede petsai, brede martin, brede malbar, brede chou chou, brede choux*, Chinese cabbage.

Preparation : 10 min • Cooking : 5 min
★ Very easy ☆ Cheap

FRESH MANGE-TOUT AND MINT SOUP

120 gm unsalted butter
1 kilo fresh mange-tout
cleaned and stringed
4 spring onions, finely chopped
700 ml chicken stock
200 ml fresh double cream
12 mint leaves
5 gm freshly ground black pepper
seasoning

4 servings

Melt 60 gm of the butter in a pan on a slow heat. Cook the mange-tout in the butter with the spring onions.

Add the chicken stock and simmer for 10 minutes until very tender.

Place the mixture into a blender. Blend on top speed until pureed, then put the mixture through a fine sieve, pressing down until the residue is quite dry.

Replace the soup into the blender and blend again at top speed. Add the rest of the ingredients. Season to taste.

Serve hot from the blender.

Note: In place of the mint, 85 gm of cooked smoked back bacon may be used.

Chop it finely, then add after the soup has been blended.

Preparation : 10 min • Cooking : 15 min
★ Very easy ☆ Cheap

Previous page: Fresh Mange-Tout & Mint Soup

SATURDAY NIGHT SOUP

oil for frying
1 large peeled onion, coarsely chopped
4 sticks stringed celery, coarsely chopped
100 gm sliced leeks
2 large peeled carrots, cut into cubes
400 gm sliced shin of beef
50 gm long grain rice
100 gm peeled potato cut into cubes
*3 large tomatoes, skinned and seeds
removed*
100 gm peeled pumpkin, cut into cubes
*100 gm cleaned cabbage
coarsely chopped*
1 bay leaf
1 litre beef stock
4 pieces bone marrow
seasoning

4 servings

Heat the oil in a pan. Fry onions until soft. Stir in the celery, leeks, and the carrots and cook for two minutes.

Add the shin of beef and cook for a further 5 minutes, turning after 2 minutes.

Add the rest of the ingredients, except the bone marrow. Bring to the boil, and allow to simmer until the rice is cooked.

Season to taste, and add the bone marrow, cook for 2 more minutes.

Pour into the serving bowl with the bone marrow on top.

Serve with Tomato and Coriander Chutney.

Preparation : 30 min • Cooking : 40 min
★ Easy   ☆ Cheap

LAMB AND CHICK PEA SOUP

1 medium leg of lamb
90 gm olive oil
2 medium onions finely chopped
*90 gm chick peas, previously soaked
and skinned*
60 gm tomato puree
½ tsp hot chilli sauce
½ tsp turmeric powder
6 fresh coriander leaves
1 cinnamon stick
6 fresh mint leaves, chopped
1 lemon squeezed for juice
shorba to taste (optional)
15 gm chopped parsley
seasoning

6 servings

Cut the meat away from the bone. Cut the lamb into bite-sized pieces.

Heat the olive oil in a pan. Cook the onions, but do not brown.

Add the meat and, on a low heat, cook for 10 minutes.

Add the chick peas and cook for further 5 minutes.

Stir in the tomato puree with a wooden spoon.

Pour in ½ litre water, chilli and the turmeric, stir in and cook for 30 minutes on a very low heat.

Add the coriander and another ½ litre water plus the cinnamon. Boil for a further 5 minutes.

Just prior to serving add the mint, lemon juice, shorba and parsley.

Season to taste.
Serve very hot.

Preparation : 20 min • Cooking : 55 min
★ Easy   ☆ Moderate

CHILLED AVOCADO SOUP

5 large avocado
1 lemon (finely grate the rind
and squeeze for the juice)
750 ml chicken stock
240 ml double cream

4 servings

Cut the avocados in half and remove the stone. Mash the flesh of 4½ avocados.

Cut into a fine dice the remaining half and toss in the lemon juice. Work quickly before the avocado turns brown. Pour the stock into a pan and bring to the boil. When just about to boil remove from the heat and whisk in the avocado puree. Stir in the grated lemon rind and salt to taste. Place in blender with the cream on top speed. Refrigerate for 4 hours. Prior to serving place the avocado into each dish then pour the soup over. Serve very cold.

Preparation : 10 min • Cooking : 10 min
★ Very easy   ☆ Moderate

OYSTER SOUP

24 oysters
100 gm unsalted butter
1 small onion, 1 small leek,
60 gm carrots, ½ stalk celery
finely chopped
100 ml dry white wine
1 branch chopped chervil
1 clove crushed garlic
1 branch fresh thyme
150 ml fresh cream
750 ml fish stock

4 servings

Open the oysters and place in a bowl, set the juice aside.

Heat 30 gm of butter on a low heat.

Cook all of the vegetables for 2 minutes taking care not to brown.

Pour in wine, fish stock, the oyster liquor and the crushed garlic and bring to the boil. Put the oysters in the boiling liquor, with thyme. Simmer for 10 minutes.

Pour into the blender, reserving 8 of the oysters. Blend for 3 minutes on top speed, pass through a fine strainer.

Replace into the blender. Blend again adding the cream and the remaining butter, melted. Season to taste.

Place two oysters in each plate and pour over the hot soup. Sprinkle with the chopped chervil.

Preparation : 25 min • Cooking : 30 min
★ Easy   ☆ Expensive

PUMPKIN AND THYME SOUP

100 gm unsalted butter
500 gm pumpkin flesh, coarsely chopped
1 medium potato, coarsely chopped
1 medium leek, coarsely chopped
1 large carrot, coarsely chopped
1 medium onion, coarsely chopped
½ stalk celery, coarsely chopped
10 gm parsley, coarsely chopped
750 ml chicken stock
2 branches fresh thyme (or ½ tsp dried)
150 ml fresh cream

4 servings

Heat 50 gm of the butter in a pan on a low heat. Add all the vegetables and cook for 2 minutes, taking care not to burn.

Add the chicken stock and the thyme and bring to the boil. Place a lid on the pan and simmer for 20 minutes.

Pour the liquor into the blender. Blend on top speed for 3 minutes. Pass through a fine sieve, and pour back in blender.

Blend again, adding the cream and the remaining butter, melted. Season.

Preparation : 20 min • Cooking : 25 min
★ Very easy   ☆ Cheap

Clockwise from top left: Chilled Avocado Soup, Pumpkin & Thyme Soup, Oyster Soup, Mulligatawny Soup (p. 42)

MULLIGATAWNY SOUP

1 cinnamon stick
3 black cardamoms
20 gm ghee
1 large cleaned onion finely chopped
500 gm chicken meat cut into small pieces
2 large cleaned chillies
1 pinch salt
4 cloves crushed garlic
5 gm ground cummin
12 leaves coriander
8 curry leaves
5 gm turmeric powder
1 bay leaf
1 litre chicken stock
20 gm plain flour
40 gm unsalted butter
1 cup coconut milk
40 gm cooked white rice
seasoning

4 servings

Crush the cinnamon and cardamom to a paste with some water.

Place the ghee in a pan on a moderate heat. Fry the onions until soft but not brown. Add the chicken and stir fry for 1 minute.

Crush the chillies with a little salt. Add the chillies and garlic to the pan and stir in. Add the rest of the spices and cook for 1 more minute.

Pour in the chicken stock and bring to the boil.

Make a paste with the flour and the butter. Whisk this into the soup. Continue boiling until of a thicker consistency.

Remove the bay leaves, curry leaves and the cinnamon stick. Season to taste.

Pour in the coconut milk and add the rice to the soup. Serve in a tureen.

Preparation : 20 min • Cooking : 20 min
★ Very easy ☆ Moderate

SPICY COCONUT SOUP

60 gm unsalted butter
1 large finely chopped onion
30 gm curry powder
250 ml chicken stock
250 ml fresh coconut milk
1 peeled green paw paw
120 gm flaked fresh coconut
250 ml double cream

4 servings

Heat the butter in a pan on a low heat. Cook the onions slowly, do not allow to colour.

Add the curry powder and fry for three minutes, stirring all the time.

Add the stock, coconut milk, paw paw and cook for a further 5 minutes until the paw paw is tender.

Place in the blender with coconut and cream and liquidize until smooth. Season.

Chill for 2 hours.

Preparation : 15 min • Cooking : 15 min
★ Easy ☆ Cheap

BREAD FRUIT SOUP

1 large bread fruit
4 medium cleaned leeks
1½ litres water
1 pinch salt
1 cup chicken stock
oil for frying
1 large onion sliced into rings
2 cloves crushed garlic
250 gm pork trimmings
150 gm watercress
½ cup fresh cream
seasoning

4 servings

Peel the bread fruit and cut into dice. Chop the leeks finely.

Boil the leeks and bread fruit in the water with a little salt. Cook for 8 minutes, or until the bread fruit is soft, and strain.

Place the leeks and bread fruit into a liquidizer and puree with the stock.

Place oil in pan and heat. Fry the onion rings and garlic until soft but do not allow to colour.

Add the pork trimmings and cook for one minute.

Put the onions and pork fat into the puree.

Remove the leaves from the watercress and add to the soup.

Allow the soup to simmer slowly for 5 minutes.

Just before serving remove the pork and stir in the cream.

Season to taste.

Preparation : 15 min • Cooking : 15 min
★ Easy ☆ Cheap

CURRIED LENTIL SOUP

500 gm lentils
1½ litres beef stock
1 ham bone
4 stalks celery
2 cloves crushed garlic
½ tsp cummin seed
20 gm curry powder
250 ml double cream
60 ml natural yoghurt
120 gm finely chopped ham
seasoning

4 servings

Soak the lentils for about 2 hours in sufficient water to cover.

Bring lentils to the boil, cook for about 15 minutes, then drain.

Add to the lentils the beef stock, ham bone, and the celery stalks in a larger saucepan.

Simmer for about 1 hour, adding more stock if necessary.

Add the garlic, cummin seed and curry powder.

Cook for a further 1½ hours.

Remove the ham bone. Puree the soup in a blender, then pour back into the saucepan.

Mix together the cream and yoghurt. Add to the lentils and cook for a further 5 minutes; season to taste.

Place the ham into a soup tureen and pour on the soup.

Preparation : 25 min • Cooking : 3 h
★ Easy ☆ Moderate

FISH BALL SOUP

2 gm spring onions
10 gm peeled, finely sliced fresh root ginger
150 gm rape or spinach leaves chopped finely
8 large Chinese black mushrooms soaked well
60 gm bamboo shoots
60 gm cucumber
210 gm boneless firm fish
1 egg white
2 tots rice wine
6 gm monosodium glutamate (optional)
1 small carrot, finely chopped
60 gm fresh beanshoots
4 lettuce leaves, finely chopped
seasoning

4 servings

Cut the spring onion into 2.5 cm pieces.

Add the sliced ginger and place into ½ cup of water. Allow to stand for 2 hours, to extract the flavour. Strain and reserve the liquid, discard the rest.

Wash the rape or spinach leaves and allow to drain. Slice the mushrooms and bamboo shoots. Peel and slice the cucumber. Finely mash the fish fillet into a paste in a bowl.

Combine the mashed fish, egg white, ½ of the rice wine, M.S.G. and ginger liquid. Divide this mixture in half and place into two separate bowls.

Place the rape or spinach leaves into a piece of muslin, squeeze a few drops of liquid from the leaves into one bowl of the fish mixture. This gives a rich green colour. Mix well.

Slowly bring 1 litre of water to boil.

Form the fish mixture into small balls. Place into the boiling water.

As each ball comes to the top scoop it out with a perforated spoon.

Cook the julienne of carrots until tender in the fish stock with the remaining rice wine. This only takes a few seconds. The carrots should still be a little crunchy in texture.

Place the fish balls, cucumber, mushrooms, bamboo shoots, beanshoots, lettuce and the carrots into a soup tureen. Pour the boiling fish stock over the above and season to taste.

Serve an equal amount of white and green fish balls.

Note: two drops of green food colouring may be used instead of the rape or spinach leaves to give the desired very pale green colour.

Preparation : 35 min • Cooking : 10 min
★ Difficult   ☆ Moderate

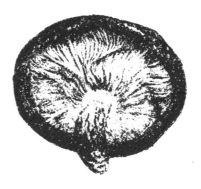

Left: Fish in Bouillon (p. 46)
Right: Fish Ball Soup

FISH IN BOUILLON

2 large tomatoes, skinned and seeded
oil for frying
1 small onion coarsely chopped
2 small cleaned green chillies
5 gm turmeric, crushed
400 gm cato or any firm white fish
cut into bite sized pieces
1 litre fish stock
12 leaves fresh coriander
2 cloves garlic, crushed
1 sprig fresh parsley
1 sprig fresh thyme
½ sprig metee leaves (optional)
12 leaves fresh coriander
2 spring onions, chopped coarsely
seasoning

4 servings

Chop the tomato flesh into pieces.

Heat the oil in a pan. Fry the onion until soft but not brown.

Stir in the tomatoes, chillies and turmeric. Add the fish and fry gently, do not allow to colour. Pour in the fish stock and bring to the boil.

Add the rest of the ingredients except the spring onions and coriander; allow to simmer for 15 minuters.

Remove the thyme, parsley and metee leaves. Season to taste.

Pour into a serving bowl. Sprinkle the coriander leaves and the spring onions on top.

Preparation : 15 min • Cooking : 25 min
★ Easy   ☆ Cheap

LOBSTER IN BOUILLON

½ litre water
10 gm salt
1 medium onion
3 cloves
1 sprig thyme
1 bay leaf
1 kilo lobster
1 small leek, cleaned
1 small carrot, cleaned
1 stick celery, cleaned
4 leaves coriander

2 servings

Bring the water to the boil with the salt.

Pierce the onion with the cloves. Place the onion, thyme and the bay leaf into the water. When the water is boiling, drop the lobster into the pot.

Shred the leeks, carrots and celery into a fine julienne.

Cook the lobster for approximately 20 minutes. Remove the pot and reduce the water by half.

Detach the tail from the head of the lobster and cut in half. Clean the duct from the tail and place the tail into a dish.

Remove the onion from the water.

Sprinkle the shredded vegetables over the lobster. Pour over the reduced stock and place the coriander leaves on top. Decorate with the head and claws and serve.

Eat the lobster first and drink the bouillon afterwards.

Preparation : 10 min • Cooking : 20 min
★ Easy   ☆ Expensive

RACON RASSAM

1 kilo songe
10 gm tamarind paste
5 cloves garlic
9 gm root ginger
8 gm aniseed
5 gm black peppercorns
2 medium onions
5 curry leaves (fresh)
2 large peeled, seeded tomatoes
4 medium green chillies
oil for frying
1 litre water
10 gm turmeric powder
500 gm cooked dholl
seasoning

6 servings

Boil the songe in water for approximately 12 minutes.

Soak the tamarind in cold water for 10 minutes to dissolve.

Liquidize or crush the garlic, ginger, aniseed and peppercorns.

When the songe is cooked, strain and keep the water apart. Crush half of the songe to a paste. Clean and chop the onions and curry leaves. Cut the tomatoes and chillies into a fine julienne.

Heat the oil in the pan. Place the liquidized ingredients into the oil. Fry gently for 5 minutes.

Add the onions, curry leaves, tomatoes turmeric and chillies. Pour the tamarind and songe water into the mixture. Add the cooked dholl. Cook for 20 minutes. Remove the curry leaves.

Before serving cut the rest of the cooked songe into a very fine dice and add, plus the songe paste. Season to taste.

If green chillies are not available use dried chillies. These can be added to the bouillon at the last minute.

Note: This is a typically Madras dish, though not as hot. For extra "fire" a tot of rum may be added before serving.

Preparation : 15 min • Cooking : 30 min
★ Easy   ☆ Cheap

HALIM

100 gm black lentils
75 gm rice
75 gm dholl or yellow split peas
200 gm unsalted butter
500 gm young goat (or lamb) meat
cut into small pieces
10 gm ground root ginger
2 large fresh chillies, crushed
1 cinnamon stick
3 elaichi seeds (cardamom)
3 cloves
10 peppercorns
1 medium onion, crushed
150 gm boiled pearl barley
16 leaves chopped fresh coriander
salt

4 servings

Cook the lentils, rice and the dholl in 2 litres of water or in a pressure cooker. When cooked puree in a blender.

Heat the butter in a pan. Cook the meat in the butter for 5 minutes. Add the spices the salt, and the onion.

Pour in 1½ litres of water and continue to cook for 10 minutes. Add the pearl barley. Add the puree of lentils, stirring often. Allow to cook for a further 20 minutes.

Before serving, sprinkle with chopped coriander leaves.

Preparation : 20 min • Cooking : 2 h
★ Easy   ☆ Moderate

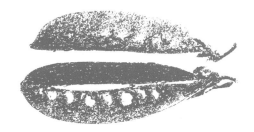

CURRY SAUCE

oil for frying
1 small onion, finely chopped
40 gm curry powder
4 medium tomatoes cut into quarters
½ litre stock
1 sprig fresh thyme
10 fresh curry leaves, finely chopped
2 sprigs fresh coriander leaves
finely chopped
3 cloves crushed garlic
15 gm crushed root ginger
4 chillies

Heat the oil in a pan.

Fry the onion until soft but not brown. Add the curry powder and stir well with a wooden spoon.

Add the tomatoes and cook for 5 minutes, stirring all the time.

Add the stock and simmer gently. Add the rest of the ingredients. Allow to cook for about 5 minutes and the stock will reduce a little and thicken.

When at the correct consistency remove from the fire.

Remove the sprig of thyme.

Note: This basic recipe can be used in many ways.
• Add the required meat plus, if required, peas and potatoes to cook in the sauce.
• Strain and put in the blender with fresh cream and add turmeric powder.
• Strain, allow to cool, mix with mayonnaise and whipped cream, serve chilled.
• Strain, allow to cool. Blend and whisk with softened butter, allow to chill. Serve with hot crusty bread.

Preparation : 10 min • Cooking : 10 min
★ Very easy   ☆ Cheap

PEANUT SAUCE FOR SEAFOOD

45 gm vegetable oil
2 medium onions
2 cloves crushed garlic
60 gm brown sugar
½ cup fresh double cream
2 cups unsalted roasted and
hulled peanuts
60 gm unsalted butter
1 large fresh chilli
finely chopped
2 limes squeezed for juice
1½ cups water

Heat the oil in a pan. Fry the onions and the garlic to soften but not to brown. Add the sugar and cook for 2 minutes to dissolve.

Place onion-garlic mixture and all the other ingredients together into a blender. Blend for about 3 minutes.

Note: This sauce is usually served chilled with calamare, prawns or any shellfish and is quite delicious and very unusual, both in flavour and texture.

Preparation : 10 min • Cooking : 10 min
★ Easy   ☆ Cheap

Clockwise from top left: Peanut Sauce, Curry Sauce; Mango Dressing with Basil (p. 54), Hollandaise Sauce (p. 50); Creole Sauce (p. 51), Red Sauce (p. 50); Chinese Garlic Sauce (p. 54), Hot Chilly Sauce (p. 51)

SAUCE HOLLANDAISE

10 gm crushed white peppercorns
80 ml water
30 ml white wine vinegar
3 egg yolks lightly beaten
250 gm unsalted butter (melted)
1 small lemon squeezed for the juice
salt

Place in a pan the peppercorns, 60 ml water and vinegar.

Set the pan on high heat and reduce by about two thirds. When reduced, remove the pan from the heat.

Whisk the egg yolks into the liquid, whisking well all the time. Add the remainder of the water, warm again, whisking continuously.

Place a pan of water on the fire to simmer. Put the pan with the sauce over the hot water. Whisk hard, making sure that the eggs do not scramble with the heat. After 8 minutes the sauce should be smooth and creamy.

Now whisk the melted butter into the egg. If the sauce is too thick, add a little warm water. Season to taste and add the lemon juice; pass through a strainer.

Note: This sauce can be used as a base.
• Add the juice of two oranges plus finely grated and blanched zest. Serve with poached fish.
• Add some blended curry sauce for rabbit.
• Chopped parsley and basil for fish.
• Add 50 gm of English mustard mixed to a paste with some white wine.
• Fresh cream whipped and folded in the last minute and serve with poached vegetables.
• For Bernaise Sauce, to the reduction add 2 finely chopped shallots, 30 gm tarragon and replace the white wine vinegar with red wine vinegar, proceed as for Hollandaise Sauce but do not strain. Serve with steak.

Preparation : 10 min • Cooking : 15 min
★ Difficult ☆ Moderate

RED SAUCE
(SAUCE ROUGE)

250 gm camaron or prawn shells
500 gm very red tomatoes
oil for frying
1 large onion, finely chopped
10 gm crushed root ginger
1 clove crushed garlic
30 gm tomato puree
1 sprig fresh thyme
10 gm fresh parsley
30 gm unsalted butter
1 tot brandy
seasoning

Crush the shells until fine. Blanch the tomatoes in hot water and remove the skin. Cut the tomatoes in half, remove the pips.

Place two cups of water in a pan and bring to the boil.

Put the crushed shells in the water and cook them until the liquid is reduced by half.

Remove from the heat.

Chop the tomatoes very fine.

Warm the oil in a pan on a low heat. Fry the onions, taking care not to colour them.

Add the garlic, ginger and the tomato puree, and stir well. Add the liquid to the shells, and cook for 2 minutes.

Stir in the chopped tomatoes and the spices, simmer for a further 3 minutes. Pass through a fine sieve.

Whisk in the butter and brandy and season to taste.

Alternatives:
• Put in the blender with 60 ml cream.
• Add port and fold in gently 180 gm of Hollandaise Sauce. Especially good with fish.

Preparation : 20 min • Cooking : 15 min
★ Difficult ☆ Expensive

CREOLE SAUCE

750 gm fresh tomatoes
oil for frying
3 large peeled and sliced onions
10 gm grated root ginger
6 cloves crushed garlic
1 sprig fresh thyme (or ¼ level tsp dried)
5 gm chopped parsley
15 chopped coriander leaves
(or ½ level tsp dried)
4 large green chillies cut lengthways
and cleaned
6 chopped spring onions

Peel and cut the tomatoes into 6 pieces each.

Place the oil in a pan and heat gently. Cook the onions in the oil. Do not allow to colour.

Combine the rest of the ingredients, except the tomatoes, with the onions and cook on a moderate heat for 3 minutes.

Add the tomatoes and simmer for 5 minutes, stirring constantly. Remove the sprig of thyme.

This sauce may be served with any meat or fish. It may also be served with pasta dishes, vegetables or cooked palm heart.

Preparation : 10 min • Cooking : 10 min
★ Very easy   ☆ Cheap

HOT CHILLI SAUCE

30 large fresh green chillies
⅛ litre olive oil
12 cloves crushed garlic
30 gm crushed root ginger
10 gm salt
⅙ litre chicken stock
4 tots dark rum

Cut the chillies in half lengthways and remove the seeds. Dried chillies may be used if fresh ones are not available. These must be soaked in boiling water for two hours.

Place all the ingredients into a blender and mix at top speed for 2 minutes. Place the mixture into a container, cover tightly and refrigerate.

The mixture will keep in the refrigerator for at least 3 weeks.

This sauce may be used as a substitute for chillies in any dish or as an additive to make a curry, or any other dish, more fiery.

Note: When handling chillies it is always best to use thin rubber gloves and take care of the eyes and nose!

Preparation : 10 min
★ Easy   ☆ Cheap

WHITE SAUCE
(SAUCE BLANCHE)

1 large cleaned onion
4 cloves
60 gm unsalted butter
30 gm plain flour
500 ml milk
1 pinch nutmeg
seasoning

Pierce the onion with the four cloves.
Mix the butter and flour together into a paste.
Place the onion and cloves into a pan with the milk and the nutmeg. Bring to the boil.

Add the butter paste to the milk, a little at a time. Beat well with a whisk to incorporate the butter.

When the sauce is thickened remove from heat. Remove the onion and clove.

If required pass through a fine sieve. Season to taste.

Note: One can put this sauce in a blender with the butter and fresh cream to make a richer sauce. When blending the sauce will become thinner.

Preparation : 10 min • Cooking : 5 min
★ Very easy ☆ Cheap

Parsley Sauce

15 gm unsalted butter
15 gm finely chopped shallots
30 gm fish trimmings
60 gm chopped parsley
150 ml fish stock
150 ml dry white wine
300 ml double cream
60 gm unsalted butter
seasoning

Melt the 15 gm of butter in a pan over a low heat. Cook the shallots until soft but do not allow to colour. Add the fish trimmings, parsley, fish stock and the white wine. Reduce the liquor by ¾.

Add the cream and cook until the sauce begins to thicken. Season to taste.

Put in the blender at top speed and add the 60 gm butter. Strain through a fine strainer.

This sauce is served with any white fish, fried or poached.

Alternatives:

· Replace the parsley with fresh basil.
· Use roquefort cheese in place of the parsley (superb with cooked palm heart).
· Use fresh tarragon instead of parsley.
· Use ½ tsp cinnamon powder and 1 tot of dry sherry to replace the parsley.

Preparation : 5 min · Cooking : 15 min
★ Easy   ☆ Moderate

Top: Dholl Pita (p. 109)
Bottom: White Sauce, Parsley Sauce

AVOCADO DRESSING WITH TOMATO AND CORIANDER

2 large ripe avocados
1 peeled tomato
1 medium finely chopped onion
¼ tsp Hot Chilli Sauce
1 tsp finely chopped fresh coriander leaves
50 ml olive oil
75 ml malt vinegar
1 pinch freshly ground black pepper
salt

Cut the avocados in half, remove the stone and the skin. Remove the seeds from the tomato and chop coarsely.

Place all the ingredients into a blender. Blend on a low speed until the mixture becomes creamy. Season to taste and chill in the refrigerator.

Serve with salad or cold seafood.

Alternative: One may remove the chilli sauce and after having blended the sauce fold in 50 ml of freshly whipped cream. This helps lighten the sauce.

Preparation : 10 min
★ Very easy   ☆ Cheap

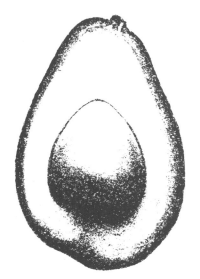

MANGO DRESSING WITH BASIL

2 large ripe mangoes
8 basil leaves
125 ml olive oil
250 ml malt vinegar
50 ml double cream
seasoning

Peel the mangoes and remove the flesh from the stone. Place all the ingredients in a blender and puree into a cream.

Season to taste and serve chilled with any salad or cold seafood.

Preparation : 10 min
★ Very easy   ☆ Cheap

CHINESE GARLIC SAUCE

1 small cleaned fresh chilli
1 pinch salt
4 cloves crushed garlic
50 ml soya sauce
50 ml vegetable oil
1 lemon squeezed for the juice
10 gm sugar
15 chopped coriander leaves
1 small spring onion finely chopped
5 ml sesame oil

Crush the chilli with the salt.

Add all the remaining ingredients and mix well.

Serve with any fried snack or Cantonese rice.

Preparation : 10 min
★ Very easy   ☆ Cheap

CRAYFISH CONSOMME WITH CORIANDER LEAVES

420 gm Crayfish or lobster
2 large leeks cleaned and diced
1 large carrot, diced
3 sticks celery, diced
4 large tomatoes, diced
1 large onion, diced
1 clove
3 litres fish stock
250 gm white fish
3 coriander stalks
1 whisked egg white
100 gm ice cubes
16 fresh coriander leaves
1 small carrot, julienned
1 small leek, julienned
1 stick celery, julienned

4 servings

Bring 2 litres of water to boil in a large pan. Plunge the crayfish into the water for 5 minutes, remove from water and allow to cool.

Remove the meat from the tails of the crayfish, retain half the meat aside for the garnish, chop the remaining crayfish into pieces.

Place the shells onto a tray into a moderate oven for about 15 minutes, remove from the oven. Take a large pan and put the shells and the rest of the meat into it.

Add half of the diced vegetables, with the clove and the fishstock. Bring to the boil and allow to simmer for approximately 45 minutes.

Skim any scum off the top at regular intervals. Pass carefully through fine muslin and allow to cool.

Mix together the white fish, the remaining diced vegetables, coriander stalks, egg whites and the ice cubes. Place this mixture into a pan with the now cold stock, mix well with a whisk and bring to the boil. Allow to gently simmer for a further 30 minutes. Again pass carefully through fine muslin, and bring to the boil

again. Season to taste with salt and pepper.

Cut the crayfish tails that have been set aside, into 16 medallions. Place 4 into each consomme cup with the very fine julienne of vegetables — pour the boiling consomme into the consomme cups and place 4 coriander leaves on top of each serving. Serve immediately.

Preparation : 20 min • Cooking 1½ h
★ Easy   ☆ Expensive

TUNA DRESSING

120 gm sour cream
180 gm fillet of fresh tuna
1 lemon squeezed for juice
15 gm curry powder
1 large green pepper, chopped
15 gm toasted sesame seeds
seasoning

1 cocktail

Place all the ingredients, with the exception of the sesame seeds, into a blender, blend until smooth, season to taste. Refrigerate the mixture.

Before serving sprinkle with toasted sesame seeds, serve with salad vegetables of your choice.

Preparation : 10 min
★ Very easy   ☆ Cheap

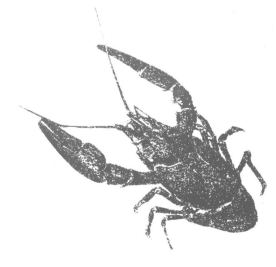

INDIAN OCEAN

HARVEST

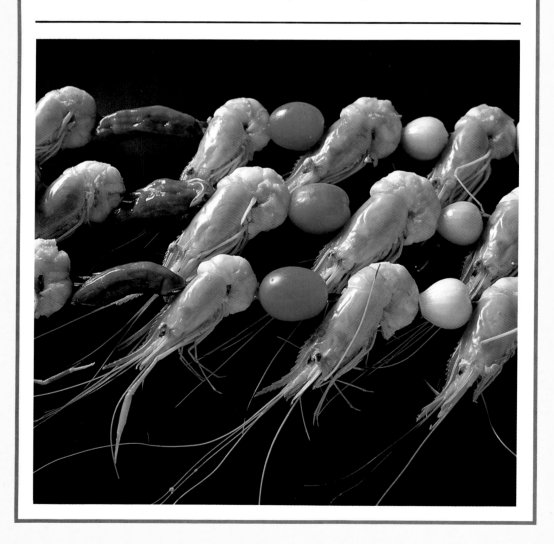

Most visitors come to Mauritius expecting to find an abundance of fish and seafood and they are not disappointed. The delicacy most highly prized by visitors, and consequently fetching the highest price, is the lobster, locally-known as the *langouste*. After a few days on the island, they come to hear about the existence of another succulent seafood, the *camaron*, sometimes also called *rosenbergi*. Reared in specialised breeding farms, mainly found on sugar estates, the *camaron* is a giant freshwater prawn that starts life in brackish water, grows up with little salt and ends up in maturity producing an unusual flavour which can be enjoyed through a variety of cooking methods — from simple to relatively complicated.

Around the Mahébourg area, off the south-east coast, one catches meaty crabs but they are fairly scarce on the market. The local inhabitants turn them into a succulent consommé, with chillies and tomatoes sometimes used with reckless abandon.

To get an idea of the true Indian Ocean harvest, one should visit the fish-landing stations dotted around the coast. Decorated with nets and floats, they are usually sited in picturesque fishing villages. Here the fishermen proudly display in their small boats (*pirogues*), their variegated catch smelling still of seaweed and invigorating brine. One is immediately taken by the wide variety of colours and patterns — from the pink *rouget* to the purple-backed flying fish, from the crimson-red *vieille-rouge* to the silver grey mullet and the metallic-skinned *cordonnier*, still fresh and iridescent.

The most succulent of all is the *sacréchien*, loosely translated as the "sacred dog", which might just carry a faint echo of the French oath *sacré nom d'un chien* meaning more or less, "by the Holy Rood". However the white tuna, caught in the deep-blue waters beyond, is a close rival, with a rich, unique flavour. The red tuna, caught mainly in March and April, has to be marinated in a mixture of grated carrots, oil, vinegar, crushed garlic, salt, pepper, thyme and white wine before grilling. *Carange* (kingfish), *vacoas* and *capitaine* are also popular and succulent fish, so too is the *daurado*, or small dolphin.

Sea urchins or *oursins* are very common in Mauritius. Normally a squeeze of lime is all you need before scooping out the roe with a teaspoon. Famous chef Michel Rostang of Paris has created a superb dish combining *oursin* and quail eggs. Octopus and calamary make very fine curries or combine well with Creole sauce.

PRAWNS WITH TAMARIND SAUCE

30 gm tamarind paste
125 ml boiling water
500 gm large peeled prawn
½ tsp Hot Chilli Sauce
2 tsp brown sugar
oil for frying

4 servings

Soak the tamarind in the boiling water to dissolve, about 20 minutes.

Make deep incisions down the back of the prawns.

Place the prawns in a bowl and pour over the strained tamarind water.

Mix in well, adding the chilli sauce and the sugar.

Allow to marinate for 1 hour.

Heat the oil in a pan on a high heat.

Drain the prawns from the liquid, keeping separate.

Cook the drained prawns for around 2 minutes.

Pour over the tamarind liquid and cook for a further 2 minutes or until the prawns are tender.

Remove the prawns and keep warm. Reduce the liquid left in the pan by two-thirds.

Place the prawns on the plate and pour the sauce over.

Serve with Delicious Rice and Hot Spicy Gherkins.

Preparation : 10 min • Cooking : 5 min
★ Easy   ☆ Expensive

PALOURDES A LA CREOLE

1 kilo palourdes or oysters
½ glass dry white wine
300 gm Creole Sauce
2 cloves crushed garlic
2 lemon

4 servings

Clean the palourde shells well before opening.

To open, place them into a pan of hot water for 5 minutes.

Remove from the shell and squeeze the lemon juice over.

Heat the Creole Sauce, add the crushed garlic and the white wine.

Add the palourdes to the sauce and cook for 2 minutes.

Serve with Creole Rice.

Preparation : 15 min • Cooking : 15 min
★ Easy   ☆ Moderate

BROCHETTE OF PRAWNS

32 king prawns
8 cleaned sweet green peppers
1 sprig fresh lemon thyme
8 peeled button onions
8 baby tomatoes
30 gm melted butter

4 servings

Allow 8 prawns per person plus two pieces of each vegetable.

Make a cut down the centre tail of the prawn with a very sharp knife.

Remove the shell from the tail, keeping tail and head intact. Clean the duct from the tail.

Cut the green pepper into 8 pieces. Remove the leaves from the sprig of thyme. Blanch the onions in boiling water for 2 minutes.

Pierce the prawn's tail and head with the skewer.

Pierce the rest of the ingredients and place alternately in between the prawns.

Season to taste and brush with the melted butter.

Grill under a moderate grill, on top of a slow barbeque or cook in a moderate oven. Serve immediately.

Preparation : 20 min • Cooking : 10 min
★ Very easy   ☆ Expensive

Previous page: Brochettes of Prawns

PRAWNS AND FISH IN GINGER PEANUT SAUCE

2 medium peeled tomatoes
75 ml olive oil
1½ kilo firm white fish fillets
cut into bite-sized pieces
500 gm cleaned prawns
1 medium finely chopped onion
½ tsp Hot Chilli Sauce
½ litre milk
150 gm freshly grated coconut
60 gm dried shrimps
2 tsp freshly chopped coriander leaves
10 gm freshly grated root ginger
20 gm cornflour diluted with water
90 gm crushed peanuts
125 ml cream

10 servings

Cut the tomatoes in half, remove seeds and chop coarsely.

Heat the oil in a pan on a moderate heat.

Cook the fish and prawns in the oil; be careful not to overcook.

When cooked remove from the pan and keep warm.

Add the onions to the pan and cook but do not allow to brown.

Stir in the tomatoes and chilli sauce; stir for 1 minute.

Then add the milk, coconut, dried shrimps, coriander and the ginger.

Bring to the boil and simmer for 10 minutes.

Stir in the cornflour and stir well until the soup starts to thicken.

Place the soup into a blender for 30 seconds, adding the cream and peanuts.

Return to the stove, add the cooked fish and prawns and simmer for 2 more minutes.

Season to taste.

Serve hot.

Preparation : 25 min • Cooking : 25 min
★ Easy ☆ Moderate

STUFFED OYSTERS

1 large cleaned onion
30 ml olive oil
60 gm fresh white button mushrooms
finely chopped
½ lemon finely grated
90 gm short grained rice
30 gm fresh pine nuts
1 pinch all spice powder
1 tblsp finely chopped lemon grass or
chervil
1 small pinch freshly ground black pepper
24 fresh oysters
2 cups water
8 lemon wedges

4 servings

Finely chop the cleaned onions.

Heat the oil in a pan. Fry the onions in the oil; be careful not to brown. Stir in the mushrooms, lemon, rice, nuts, spice and the pepper, cook for one minute and remove from the heat. Keep to one side.

Take the oysters and scrub the shells until clean. If necessary, scrap any foreign bodies off the oysters shells with a knife. Open the oysters, taking care not to separate the shells.

Place two teaspoons of filling into the shell. Close the shell again.

Place the oysters in a dish. Rest another heavy dish on top to prevent the oysters from opening during cooking.

Pour in the water and the lemon grass. Bring the water to the boil and then turn the heat down to simmer. Cook for about 30 minutes, taking a look at the water level regularly. Top up if necessary.

When ready remove the pan from the heat and allow to cook for 10 minutes.

Remove the oysters from the pan.

Wipe the shells with a cloth dipped in a little oil. (This is solely for appearance).

Arrange on a serving dish with lemon wedges.

Preparation : 25 min • Cooking : 50 min
★ Difficult ☆ Expensive

CRAYFISH SAINT GERAN SUN

1 × 700 gm boiled crayfish or lobster
1 large avocado pear
lemon squeezed for the juice
1 egg yolk
1 pinch nutmeg
40 ml double cream
150 gm unsalted butter
120 gm blanched spinach leaves
1 small finely chopped onion
150 gm cleaned, sliced mushrooms
60 ml white sauce
1 sprig fresh thyme
90 gm grated cheese
1 tot Pernod, olives
salt

2 servings

Detach the tail from the head of the crayfish. Cut the tail in half, remove the flesh and clean the duct. Cut the flesh into bite-sized pieces.

Cut the avocado pear in half and remove the stone. With a parisienne cutter cut the avocado into ball shapes, sprinkle with the lemon juice and set aside. Add the egg yolk and nutmeg to the cream and whisk together.

Put 30 gm of butter in a pan on a low heat. Toss the cooked spinach leaves in the butter, do not overcook. Remove from the pan and keep warm. Place the rest of the butter in the pan, again on a low heat.

Cook the chopped onions, but do not allow to colour. Add the sliced mushrooms and cook for one minute. Blend the crayfish pieces in with mushrooms and onions. Heat for 1 minute.

Pour in the white sauce and the thyme. Stir continuously to heat through.

Pour in the egg and cream mixture and fold into the sauce and crayfish. Remove the pan from the heat and season to taste. Stir in 20 gm of the cheese plus the Pernod. Remove the thyme.

Place the warm spinach in the base of the crayfish tails. Spoon the crayfish into the tails, dividing the flesh equally. Sprinkle the remaining cheese on top and place under a hot grill until golden.

Place the crayfish on a plate and decorate with the avocado and olives.

Preparation : 1 h • Cooking : 25 min
★ Difficult   ☆ Expensive

CRAYFISH IN BOUILLON

½ litre water
1 medium onion
3 cloves
1 sprig thyme
1 bay leaf
1 kilo crayfish
1 small leek cleaned
1 small carrot cleaned
1 stick celery cleaned
4 leaves fresh coriander

2 servings

Bring the water to the boil with salt. Pierce the onion with cloves and place with thyme and bay leaf into the water.

When the water is boiling, drop the crayfish into the pot. Shred the leeks, carrots and celery into a fine julienne. Cook the crayfish for 20 minutes. Remove from the pot and reduce the water by half. Detach the tail from the head of the crayfish and cut in half. Clean the duct from the tail and place the tail into a dish. Remove the onion from the water.

Sprinkle the shredded vegetables over the crayfish. Pour over the reduced stock and place the coriander leaves on top.

Decorate with the head and claws.

Eat the crayfish first and drink the bouillon afterwards.

Preparation : 10 min • Cooking : 20 min
★ Easy   ☆ Expensive

Top: Crayfish Saint Géran Sun
Bottom: Crayfish in Bouillon

FRICASSEE OF SEAFOOD

300 gm fillet of white fish
cut into bite-sized pieces
20 oysters out of the shell
5 scallops out of the shell
300 gm crab meat
300 gm cleaned prawns
1 lemon squeezed for the juice
½ sprig fresh thyme
1 celery stick, chopped
1 medium onion, chopped
3 medium green peppers, chopped
30 gm unsalted butter
4 rashers streaky bacon
cut into small pieces
1 clove garlic crushed
30 gm plain flour
1 cup dry white wine
200 ml fresh double cream
1 tot Ricard
chopped parsley
seasoning

5 servings

Place seafood into 1 litre of boiling water with the lemon and thyme. Boil quickly for 3 minutes and strain the fish from the liquor. Set aside. Reduce the fish stock by half by boiling.

Cook the vegetables with the bacon and a little butter in a pan. Do not allow to brown.

Add the crushed garlic and stir well. Add the flour and stir in, mixing very well with a wooden spoon. Pour in the white wine and the reduced stock, stir well, cooking for 10 minutes.

Gently add the seafood, fresh cream, Ricard and the chopped parsley.

Sprinkle with chopped parsley and serve with Creole Rice.

Preparation : 20 min • Cooking 20 min
★ Easy   ☆ Moderate

SMOKED MARLIN WITH QUAIL EGGS AND HORSERADISH AND MINT CREAM

8 slices smoked marlin
(or smoked salmon)
8 fresh quail eggs
30 gm horseradish relish
10 leaves fresh mint
20 ml fresh double cream
6 leaves crisp lettuce
12 thin slices cleaned cucumber

4 servings

Boil the quail eggs for 3 minutes in water until hard boiled.

Run under cold water for 5 minutes. This stops a black ring from forming around the yolk.

Remove the shells from the eggs and cut the eggs in half.

Take the relish, mint leaves and the fresh cream.

Place into a liquidiser and blend until of a creamy consistency.

Keep in the refrigerator until ready to use.

On 4 plates place the lettuce and the cucumber slices.

Place the marlin over the salad and then the eggs on top of the marlin, 4 halves per plate.

Gently cover the eggs and the marlin with the blended cream.

Serve alone.

Preparation : 20 min • Cooking : 4 min
★ Easy   ☆ Expensive

OCTOPUS IN A CHEESE SAUCE GRATIN

1 kilo fresh octopus, cleaned
1 medium onion, finely chopped
3 cloves crushed garlic
1 sprig fresh thyme
1 large cleaned chilli
2 glasses white wine
50 gm white breadcrumbs
90 gm cheddar cheese (grated)
250 ml fresh cream
20 gm parmesan cheese
30 gm unsalted butter (melted)
seasoning

4 servings

Cut the octopus into bite-sized pieces.

In a pan place the octopus, onion, garlic, thyme, chilli, salt and wine. Cover with water and cook for 5 minutes or until the octopus is tender.

Mix the breadcrumbs and cheddar cheese together.

When the octopus is tender strain it from the broth and keep warm. Replace the broth into a pan. Reduce the broth by three quarters.

Add the cream and parmesan cheese. Allow to cool for a further 10 minutes. The mixture should begin to thicken.

Place the octopus in a dish. Pour over the sauce. Sprinkle over the top the cheese and breadcrumb mixture with the melted butter.

Place under the grill and brown.

Preparation : 10 min • Cooking : 1h 10 min
★ Easy   ☆ Moderate

CRAB JHISLAINE

4 large crabs
oil for frying
1 medium finely chopped onion
2 cloves crushed garlic
1 sprig fresh thyme
1 bay leaf
1 medium crushed chilli
1 pinch paprika
juice of one lemon
seasoning

4 servings

Clean the crab and remove the meat from the shell.

Cut the flesh into pieces.

Place the oil in a pan on a moderate heat.

Put the crab into the heated oil and cook for 2 minutes.

Pour over just sufficient water to cover the crab meat.

Add the rest of the ingredients and stir in.

Cook for 5 minutes or until the water evaporates.

Remove the sprig of thyme and bay leaf.

Replace the cooked crab into the cleaned crab shell.

Serve instantly with Creole Rice and Chevrette, coconut, or Tomato and Coriander chutneys.

Preparation : 20 min • Cooking : 10 min
★ Easy   ☆ Expensive

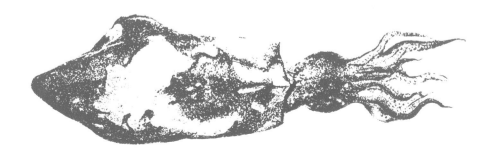

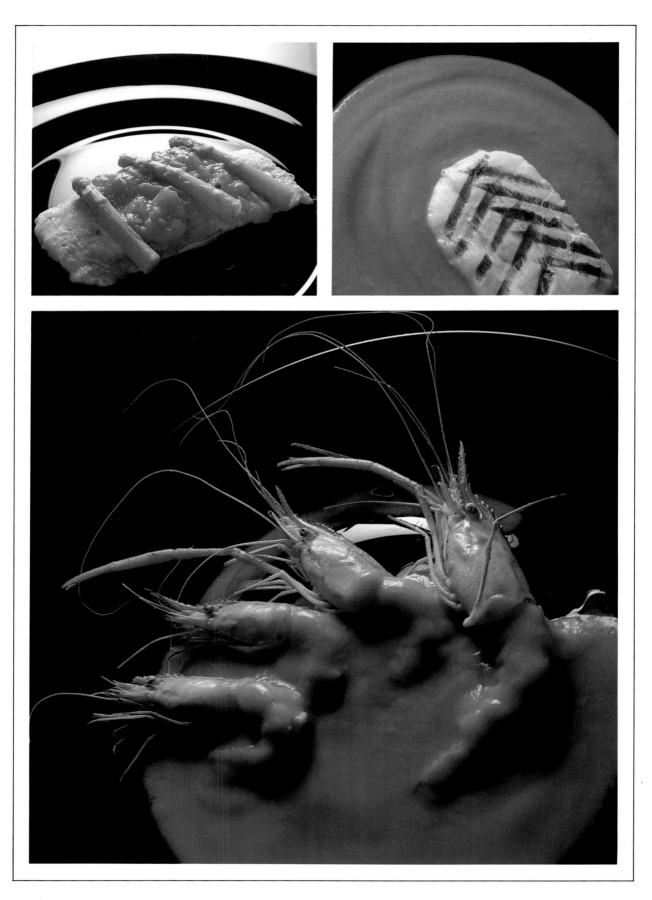

CAMARONS IN RED SAUCE

12 large camarons or king prawns
1 large onion
½ kg very red tomatoes
3 cloves crushed garlic
5 gm crushed root ginger
2 tblsp tomato paste
1 sprig fresh thyme (or ¼ level tsp dried)
10 gm parsley
hard boiled egg

3 servings

Cook the camarons in a little water for a few seconds or until they become red and are cooked. Do not overcook.

Remove the shells from the camarons' tails leaving the heads intact. Place the shells on a *roche carri* and crush well, or place in a blender on low speed. Place two cups of water in a pan to boil with the crushed camaron shells. Reduce until there is 1 cup of liquid. Place in a blender on top speed for 30 seconds. Strain this mixture through a piece of muslin until dry. Put this sauce to one side. Blanch the tomatoes in boiling water and remove the skins and seeds. Chop very finely. Place the oil in a pan and heat. Clean and chop the onions very finely. Fry the onions taking care not to brown them. Add the garlic, ginger and tomato paste and stir in well. Fry for half a minute. Add the camaron sauce to the onion and tomato mixture. Blend in the chopped tomatoes and stir well. Add the thyme and parsley and cook on a low heat for 5 minutes.

Place the shelled camarons into the sauce and cook for a further 5 minutes on a gentle heat. Serve with rice and the sliced hard boiled egg.

Preparation : 15 min • Cooking 10 min
★ Difficult   ☆ Expensive

Opposite, top left: Fillet of Sacrechien Guylaine (p. 66), top right: Fillet of Kapitan à la Créole (p. 66)
Opposite, bottom: Camarons in Red Sauce
Right: Mauritian Calamary

MAURITIAN CALAMARY

500 gm cleaned calamary
8 Chinese mushrooms
60 gm bamboo shoots
30 gm young corn shoots
60 gm unsalted butter
60 gm mange-tout
1 tsp dark soya sauce
30 gm bean sprouts
30 gm grated carrots

4 servings

Use fresh calamary whenever possible as frozen tends to become tough when cooked. Cut the cleaned calamary into 3 mm strips. Cook in seasoned boiling water until tender. Drain and dry.

Soak the Chinese mushrooms in water for 10 minutes. When soft, cut into strips.

Cut the bamboo shoots into strips. Cut the young corn into four, lengthways.

Heat the oil and butter together over a moderate heat. Cook calamary for 2 minutes.

Add the mange-tout and cook for a further 2 minutes. Add the rest of the ingredients and stir-fry for 1 minute. Serve with Delicious Rice.

Preparation : 25 min • Cooking : 10 min
★ Very easy   ☆ Moderate

FILLET OF KAPITAN A LA CREOLE

*500 gm fillet of kapitan or any other
firm white fish
oil for frying
300 gm Creole Sauce
seasoning*

4 servings

Modern style:
Season the fish on both sides.

Heat the oil in a pan over a moderate heat, season and cook the fish to the desired degree.

Remove the fish from the pan and keep warm.

Heat the Creole Sauce in the pan. Liquidise and pour onto a plate. Place the fish on top and serve.

Traditional style:
Use fillet or, more usually, fish left on the bone. Season the fish.

Heat the oil in a pan on a moderate heat. Cook the fish to the desired degree; traditionally the fish is usually cooked very well.

Fry 4 chopped shallots (green part only) in the pan for ½ minute. Pour in the Creole Sauce and mix with the fish to heat through.

Serve with Creole Rice.

Preparation : 10 min • Cooking : 15 min
★ Very easy   ☆ Cheap

FILLET OF SACRE CHIEN GUYLAINE

*4 fillets of sacrechien
30 gm unsalted butter
½ glass dry white wine
1 juice of one lemon
12 green asparagus tips
120 gm Creole Sauce
90 gm Bernaise Sauce
seasoning*

4 servings

Season the fish.

Heat the butter in a pan on a low heat. Place the fish in the butter to cook for 2 minutes.

Turn the fish over to cook the other side for a further two minutes.

Add the white wine and continue cooking the fish. When finally cooked remove from pan onto a plate and keep warm. Pour the lemon juice over the fish.

Place the heated asparagus tips spaced apart on top of the fish, three pieces to each fillet of fish.

Heat the Creole Sauce in pan. Spoon the hot sauce in between the asparagus tips.

Cover the whole fish with Sauce Bernaise and place under the grill to brown.

Serve with assorted vegetables.

Preparation : 15 min • Cooking : 15 min
★ Easy   ☆ Moderate

VINDAYE OF TUNA

20 gm mustard seed
10 gm crushed root ginger
3 small green chillies
2 cloves garlic
¼ litre malt vinegar
oil for frying
5 × 120 gm fillets of tuna
20 cleaned shallots
1 large onion cleaned and chopped
10 gm turmeric
1 sprig fresh thyme
seasoning

5 servings

Crush the mustard seeds.

Crush half the garlic with the root ginger, leaving the rest of the garlic whole.

Cut the chillies in half lengthways and remove the seeds.

Add the crushed ginger, garlic and mustard to the vinegar.

Place the oil in a pan and bring to a moderate heat.

Season the fish and place it in the oil.

When cooked, remove from the pan and fry the shallots and chopped onions.

Add the whole garlic.

Stir the turmeric and thyme with the onion mixture.

Add the vinegar, mix, and stir well.

Cook for 3 minutes and season to taste.

Remove from the fire and place the fish into the sauce.

Add the chillies.

Note: This dish is most delicious when served cold with Creole Rice and various chutneys.

Vindaye can also be made with octopus and venison.

Keeping it in the refrigerator for two days improves the flavour and brings out the taste of the spices.

Preparation : 20 min • Cooking : 15 min
★ Easy   ☆ Cheap

SACRE CHIEN TROPICAL STYLE

4 × 120 gm cleaned sacrechien
or other firm white fish
½ cleaned and diced
small pineapple
seasoning
100 gm unsalted butter
30 ml fresh cream
30 gm diced cucumber
1 small diced apple
15 fresh stoneless cherries
5 gm grated ginger
3 chopped mint leaves
4 halves of lemon

4 servings

Season the fish.

Melt 30 g of the butter in a pan on a moderate heat. Fry the fish; do not allow to colour.

Take the fish out of the pan and keep warm.

Melt the rest of the butter in the pan until hot, and whisk in the fresh cream. Add the diced cucumber, fruit, ginger and mint leaves.

Place the hot fish on a platter. Spoon the garnish and butter mix over the fish. Serve with halves of lemon.

Note: Filleted fish may also be used.

Preparation : 25 min • Cooking : 10 min
★ Easy   ☆ Moderate

ROUGET IN BANANA LEAF

2 large lemons
120 gm unsalted butter
banana leaf (or aluminium foil)
4 medium whole rouget or trout
½ cup dry white wine, thyme

4 servings

Peel the two lemons, removing the pith completely and cut each of them into 6 slices.

Melt the butter.

Clean the rouget, leaving whole.

Cut the banana leaf into squares big enough to wrap the fish. Brush the banana leaf and also the fish with the melted butter. Place the fish onto the banana leaf.

Top with 3 lemon slices.

Place the ½ sprig of thyme inside each fish with a little of the wine, season and wrap the fish in the banana leaf.

Place on a buttered tray, cover over the banana parcels with foil. Cook in 250°F oven for 10 minutes.

Preparation : 10 min • Cooking : 10 min
★ Easy   ☆ Moderate

Bottom: Vacoas Père Laval
Top: Fillet of Sacrechien Trou d'Eau Douce (p. 71)
Opposite: Rouget in Banana leaf

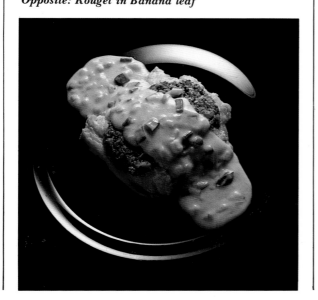

VACOAS PERE LAVAL

4 servings

20 gm unsalted butter
4 fillets of vacoas (or any firm white fish)
2 cloves crushed garlic
1 sprig thyme
1 bay leaf
1 glass white wine
1 glass fish stock
½ medium finely chopped onion
1 medium sliced carrot
1 celery stick chopped
1 leek chopped
4 black peppercorns
seasoning

In this recipe fish is topped with a mushroom duxelle, browned, and served with a whole wine sauce. See overleaf for duxelle and sauce recipes.

Brush a tray with the melted butter. Place the fillets of fish onto the tray, then add the rest of the ingredients to the fish.

Cover with oiled greaseproof paper or foil and cook for approximately 10 minutes in a pre-heated oven.

When cooked, remove from the oven and take the fish from the stock. Keep separate and keep warm.

(Following next page)

Vacoas Père Laval (following)

Sauce Davos:
60 gm unsalted butter
1 small finely chopped onion
2 glasses dry white wine
120 gm unsalted butter, softened
seasoning

Melt the butter in a pan. Cook the onions for 1 minute until soft but not brown.

Add the white wine and reduce by ⅓. Remove from the heat and allow to cool.

Whisk in slowly but briskly the remaining butter, soft but not melted. Season to taste. Be careful as the sauce can easily separate. Remove the fish from the tray and carefully pat dry.

Spread the duxelle over the top of each fillet of fish. Brush with melted butter.

Place under a very hot grill to brown.

Put the fish onto a hot platter.

Pour sauce around the fish and serve immediately, accompanied with vegetables and boiled potatoes.

Preparation : 40 min • Cooking : 25 min
★ Difficult   ☆ Moderate

Duxelle:
1 clove garlic
60 gm unsalted butter
150 gm finely chopped oinons
150 gm finely chopped
white button mushrooms
1 tot port
1 tot brandy
seasoning

Crush the garlic very well.

Heat the butter in a pan. Cook the onions and crushed garlic for 1 minute; do not allow to brown.

Add the mushrooms and cook for 2 minutes.

Stir in the rest of the ingredients and stir-fry for 3 minutes.

Season to taste and remove from the heat.

STEAMED SARDINES WITH GINGER

12 fresh sardines
2 lemons, squeezed for the juice
45 gm sugar
5 tsp soya sauce
10 gm finely grated root ginger
6 fresh coriander leaves
seasoning

4 servings

Clean and scale the sardines, steam in a Chinese steamer for 5 minutes.

Place the rest of the ingredients together in a pan, simmer for 1 minute.

Place sardines onto a plate and spoon over the sauce.

Garnish with coriander leaves if desired.

Preparation : 20 min • Cooking : 8 min
★ Very easy   ☆ Cheap

FILLET OF SACRECHIEN TROU D'EAU DOUCE

4 × 150 gm fillets of sacrechien
or other firm white fish
1 cup dry white wine
1 sprig fresh thyme
1 bay leaf
1 tsp malt vinegar
250 gm unsalted butter
2 medium bananas
juice of 1 lemon
60 gm flaked almonds
60 gm chopped cucumber
seasoning

4 servings

Remove all the bones from the fish fillets, season with salt and pepper.

Place the wine, thyme, bay leaf, vinegar and 100 gm of the butter in a pan. Place the fish in this liquor. Cover with buttered greaseproof paper. Simmer gently for 4 minutes.

When the fish is cooked, take it off the heat and remove from the liquor, keeping warm.

Peel and chop the bananas.

Place the rest of the butter into a pan on a fast fire. Cook the butter until a light nut-brown. Take off the heat immediately and pour in the lemon juice.

Cook the almonds in the butter-lemon mixture until a very light brown. Add the banana and cucumber.

Place the hot fish onto a platter and pour the sauce over it.

Serve with lemon slices and parsley.

Preparation : 20 min • Cooking : 10 min
★ Easy   ☆ Moderate

ROUGAILLE OF SALTED FISH WITH BLACK LENTILS

125 gm salted fish
oil for frying
250 ml Creole Sauce
400 gm coriander rice (cooked rice with chopped coriander)
4 servings black lentils
margoze

4 servings

Boil a pan of water and remove from the fire. Add the salted fish to the water and allow to soak for 10 minutes.

Remove the fish from the water and pat dry. Flake the fish into small pieces, removing any bones and skin at the same time.

Heat a little oil in a pan. Fry the salted fish in the oil for 2 minutes only. Remove from the pan and keep warm.

Heat the Creole Sauce and add the salted fish. Serve with the coriander rice and Black Lentils.

Note: This is served with *margoze* (a local green vegetable).

Scrape and clean the *margoze*. Cut the vegetable into two. Remove the pips and cut into fine slices. Add sea salt to the slices and rub in well. Allow to stand for 10 minutes.

Wash off the salt. Add the *margoze* to the Creole Sauce and cook in the sauce. Add the fish to the sauce.

It can also be served with:
• fricassee of haricots rouge
• fricassee of red lentils
• dholl

Preparation : 20 min • Cooking 15 min
★ Easy   ☆ Cheap

71

THRILL

OF THE CHASE

Most sugar estates in Mauritius have devoted large tracts of their territory, normally hilly scrubland with deep ravines, to enable deer to breed in the wild on fairly decent pastures and without too much out-of-season interference.

The shooting season lasts from June to October, during which time a carefully-controlled number of deer are shot during hunting parties. The meat is later shared amongst the invitees and other participants, who are usually paid members of the Society running the *chasse*, with the surplus on the local market.

The male deer is the most sought-after prize, for the impressive antlers are usually proudly displayed on the walls of colonial mansions. There is keen competition amongst the different *chassés* for the largest pair of antlers of the season.

The deer hunters normally sit on small raised wooden platforms, called *mirodors*, which give a good, wide view. The beaters than set about their work of driving the deer within range of the *miradors*. They drive them out of the thicket into the open ground which comprises alternating bushes and grassland.

Wild boar or "*cochon marron*", usually leaner than pork, is also a tasty game dish which is highly prized by Mauritians. It is served with a *purée d'arouille*, which is cooked in milk to reduce its glutinous propensities and flavoured, at the very last, with a tot of cognac.

Salade de palmiste is also a perfect companion and the whole preparation is rounded off with a *gelée de goyave de chine* — Chinese guava jelly, home-made from a local variety of red-and-yellow small guavas, grown wild here and just requiring to be picked, and standing as well for the equivalent of redcurrant jelly.

Elsewhere, in the wilds of Mauritius, one finds hare, rabbit, guinea fowl, some pheasant and quail. However, the traditions of "hanging" the meat prior to cooking are not followed here, mainly because of deterioration in the subtropical temperatures.

Fortunately, we do still find in Mauritius free-range poultry which definitely have an infinitely superior flavour to that of the battery-reared variety, especially if corn is included in their diet. The very best are imported from Rodrigues, a Mauritius "dependency", where the poultry are fed on very young corn.

Local gourmets, therefore, look forward with relish to the winter months, during which they can feast on the results of the "*chasse*".

ROAST WILD BOAR

1 cleaned wild boar (about 4 kilos)
2 cups malt vinegar
1 cinnamon stick
200 ml oil
500 gm tomato (peeled and seeded)
3 cloves garlic
2 large peeled onions
36 cloves
2 sprigs fresh thyme
2 wine glasses red wine
4 celery sticks

10 servings

Wash the boar with the vinegar. This removes some of the "gamey" taste.

Crush the cinnamon stick with a little oil and water to form a paste. Crush the tomato flesh into a paste. Crush the garlic and onions together into a paste. Mix all of the ingredients together, adding the oil.

Pierce the skin of the boar and place the cloves all over, pushing well into the skin. Cover the boar with the paste and marinate for 3 hours in an oven dish.

Pre-heat the oven to medium (350°F. 180°C) Place the boar in the oven with the celery sticks. Baste often whilst cooking.

When cooked (about 2 hours), remove from the oven. Skim the oil off the residue.

Add the red wine and some water to the residue. Mix well and bring to the boil. Serve with the boar.

Preparation : 20 min • Cooking : 2 h
★ Difficult   ☆ Expensive

Previous page: Chicken Cutlet (p. 78)

VENISON STEAK IN PEPPER SAUCE

¼ cup olive oil
1 large cleaned chopped onion
2 cleaned leeks
100 gm venison (or beef) bones
2 medium cleaned chopped carrots
20 gm tomato puree
750 ml strong beef stock
1 celery stick, chopped
2 bay leaves
10 gm parsley
125 ml malt vinegar
20 gm crushed peppercorns
125 ml red wine
10 gm green peppercorns
4 × 150 venison steaks (or fillets of beef)
60 gm unsalted butter
75 ml fresh cream

4 servings

Place the olive oil in a pan to heat. Brown the onion, leeks, bones and carrots in the oil. Add the tomato puree and stock. Stir well. Add the celery, bayleaf, parsley, cover with a lid and simmer for 1½ hours. Remove the lid and skim off any excess fat.

Mix together the vinegar, crushed peppercorns, red wine and green peppercorns. Place in a separate pan and reduce until half its original volume, then strain.

Pour the reduced vinegar and red wine mix into the sauce. Add the fresh cream and whisk in the softened butter. Simmer for a further 20 minutes.

Season to taste.

Cook the venison steak in a little oil. Remove from the pan and place on to a dish.

Pour over the sauce and serve hot.

Note: Red currant jelly can be added to this sauce for extra flavour.

Preparation : 30 min • Cooking : 2 h
★ Easy   ☆ Expensive

VENISON LIVER

500 gm venison liver (or ox liver)
2 cups red wine
20 gm green peppercorns
60 gm mushrooms
90 gm unsalted butter
1 small minced onion
juice of one lemon

4 servings

The liver of the venison must be really fresh. Slice it very thinly.

Put into the red wine and peppercorns for 3 hours to marinate.

Slice the mushrooms.

Melt the butter in a pan and fry the onion for 1 minute.

Place the liver in the pan and cook each side for about 1 minute. Remove the liver and keep warm.

Cook the sliced mushrooms in the same pan with hot butter. Into the same hot pan add the red wine and peppercorn marinade and stir well, simmering until reduced by half. Add the lemon juice.

Place the liver in the sauce and heat briefly. Serve immediately.

Note: Red currant jelly may be added to the sauce if desired.

Preparation : 5 min • Cooking : 10 min
★ Easy   ☆ Moderate

VENISON SALMIS

1 large fresh green chilli
1 sprig fresh parsley
1 sprig fresh thyme
1 cinnamon stick
3 cloves garlic
10 gm root ginger
3 cloves
30 ml oil
2 large cleaned onions
cut into slices
600 gm venison steak
cut into slices
2 wine glasses red wine
250 gm fresh tomatoes
crushed to a puree

4 servings

Crush together the chillies, parsley, thyme, cinnamon, garlic, ginger and the cloves.

Heat the oil in a pan on a moderate heat. Fry the onions for 1 minute.

Add the meat and cook in the oil for about 5 minutes, turning over often.

Into the pan add the tomato puree. Add the crushed spices and stir in well. Pour in half of the red wine and cook until the meat is tender.

Prior to serving, add the remaining red wine and season to taste.

Serve with a green salad and Bulgare Salad.

Preparation : 20 min • Cooking : 30 min
★ Easy   ☆ Expensive

VENISON CREOLE STYLE

1 large onion
500 gm boneless venison (or beef)
15 gm flour
1 litre venison stock
60 gm tomato puree
3 cloves crushed garlic
2 tsp ground cumin
5 gm ground nutmeg
2 small bananas
2 tots brandy
2 tots port

4 servings

Peel and chop the onions finely.

Cut the venison into bite-sized pieces. Sprinkle the flour onto venison with the seasoning. Heat the oil in a pan on a moderate heat. Fry the chopped onions in the oil for 1 minute. Do not brown. Add the venison and cook for a further 4 minutes. Stir in the tomato puree and cook for 1 minute. Add the crushed garlic, cumin and nutmeg, pour in the venison stock and stir well; the flour will thicken the stock as it cooks. Simmer the venison, stirring often, for 30 minutes. Check if the stock has reduced too much or sauce is too thick. If required, add more stock. Peel and slice the bananas. When the venison is tender, add the bananas and fold in. Keep the banana slices whole; do not break while stirring. Before serving, pour in the brandy and port. Season to taste.

Serve with Creole Rice.

Grated coconut may be sprinkled on top of the venison.

Preparation : 20 min • Cooking : 40 min
★ Difficult   ☆ Expensive

Top right: Breast of Chicken with Mango & Coconut (p. 79)
Top left: Chicken Toukrah
Bottom: Venison Creole Style

CHICKEN TOUKRAH

250 gm boneless chicken meat
4 large hard boiled eggs, peeled
10 ml yellow colouring
1 large potato peeled and cut into cubes
120 gm plain yoghurt
10 leaves fresh mint, finely chopped
10 leaves fresh coriander, finely chopped
3 cloves crushed garlic
1 tsp finely grated root ginger
1 cinnamon stick
4 cloves
1 large peeled finely sliced onion
1 tsp turmeric
1 large cleaned fresh chilli
finely chopped
3 bay leaves
90 gm ghee
5 gm anis seed
oil for deep frying

4 servings

Cut the chicken into bite-sized pieces.

Take the hard boiled egg and roll in the yellow colouring. Deep fry the egg for two minutes.

Do the same with the potato.

Marinate the chicken in a saucepan with the rest of the ingredients. Leave for 6 hours in the refrigerator.

Remove from the refrigerator and leave for 1 hour at room temperature.

Preheat the oven to moderate.

Place everything into a pan on a low heat and stir with a wooden spoon. Bring to the boil carefully stirring all the time. As soon as it comes to the boil, put a lid on the pot and place into the oven. Leave for 20 minutes. Or a little longer until cooked.

Serve with white rice and cucumber and mint chutney.

Preparation : 30 min • Cooking : 35 min
★ Difficult   ☆ Moderate

CHICKEN CUTLET

4 chicken legs
62 gm plain yoghurt
30 gm fresh coriander leaves
finely chopped
1 medium onion finely chopped
90 gm tomato, peeled, seeded
and crushed
5 gm finely grated root ginger
60 gm plain flour
2 large eggs beaten with a little salt
white breadcrumbs
oil for deep frying

4 servings

Cut the thigh bone from the chicken.

Open out the meat from the bone. Scrape the meat down from the drumstick towards the thigh, so that bone is left clean at one end and all the meat is forced to the other.

Mix together the yoghurt, coriander, onion, tomato and ginger. Marinate the chicken in this mixture for 12 hours.

Remove chicken from the marinade and dust with flour. Dip into the beaten egg. Roll into the breadcrumbs to cover.

Heat the oil to moderate heat and cook the chicken until golden brown.

Preparation : 30 min • Cooking : 5 min
★ Easy   ☆ Cheap

CHICKEN TIKKA

750 gm chicken breast meat
1 medium onion, chopped fine
3 cloves garlic, crushed
15 gm white vinegar
60 gm plain yoghurt
10 gm Hot Chilli Sauce
10 gm crushed coriander seeds
8 gm crushed cummin
5 gm crushed turmeric
15 gm garam masala
2 lemons squeezed for juice
salt to taste

8 tikkas

Cut the chicken into 2.5 cm pieces. Flatten just a little.

Place the rest of the ingredients except the lemon juice into a blender. Blend at slow speed for 3 minutes.

Remove mixture from the blender and place into a container. Rub the chicken pieces well with this mixture and marinate for three hours.

Thread this marinated chicken onto skewers and season with salt.

Place under a hot grill or on to a charcoal barbeque and cook until tender.

Sprinkle with the lemon juice and serve on a bed of lettuce surrounded with onion rings and lemon wedges.

Preparation : 15 min • Cooking : 10 min
★ Easy   ☆ Moderate

CHICKEN VINDALOO

1 kilo chicken meat
300 gm small potatoes
1 large finely chopped onion
4 cloves crushed garlic
10 fresh curry leaves
10 gm crushed coriander seeds
5 gm crushed root ginger
90 gm curry powder
1 large fresh cleaned and crushed chilli
50 ml natural yoghurt
oil for frying, salt
3 medium tomatoes, skinned, seeded
10 gm turmeric
250 ml water
10 fresh coriander leaves chopped
5 servings

Cut the chicken and the tomato flesh into bite-sized pieces.

Scrub the potatoes and boil in their skins until firm, but not soft; allow to cool. Peel the skin off the potatoes and cut them in half.

Mix the onions, garlic, curry leaves, crushed coriander seeds and the ginger together. Add the curry powder, chilli and the yoghurt. Mix well and set one third of this mixture aside. Into this ⅓ part fold in the potatoes. Allow to marinate for 2 hours. Heat the oil on a moderate heat. Cook the chicken in the oil for 2 minutes.

Remove from the pan, set aside and keep warm. Add the rest of the curry mixture to the hot oil. Cook for 3 minutes, stirring continually to prevent burning. Add the cooked chicken pieces to the pan. Cook for a further 5 minutes. Allow this also to stand for about 2 hours. After standing replace on the heat and stir in the tomatoes and the turmeric. Pour in the water and allow to simmer on a low heat for 5 minutes.

Add the potatoes in their mixture carefully. Mix them in with the chicken and add the coriander leaves. Heat through and serve with Pilaw Rice.

Season to taste and serve with Tomato and Coriander Chutney.

Note: If necessary more water may be added during the cooking.

Preparation : 25 min • Cooking 2 h 30 min
★ Difficult ☆ Moderate

BREAST OF CHICKEN WITH MANGO AND COCONUT

120 gm freshly grated coconut flakes
60 gm white breadcrumbs
1 mango cut into small dice
1 tot dark rum
4 boned chicken breasts
60 gm plain flour
1 large egg beaten with a pinch of salt
90 gm unsalted butter
30 ml cooking oil
seasoning
4 servings

Mix half of the coconut with the breadcrumbs.

Mix the mango together with the rum, leave for 1 hour.

Cut the chicken breasts open lengthwise, making sure you do not cut right through. Stuff the breasts with the mango and close the cut.

Lightly dust the chicken with the flour. Dip the breasts into the egg, drain and then roll into the breadcrumb mixture.

Heat the butter in a pan with the oil on a low heat. Slowly cook the breasts in the butter and oil to a golden brown.

Remove the chicken and brown the coconut in the same pan.

Serve the chicken on a plate and garnish with the rest of the coconut.

Serve with a Light Curry Sauce.

Note: Dessicated coconut steeped in milk for 1½ hours, drained well, may be used if fresh coconut is not available. Then proceed as above.

Preparation : 15 min • Cooking : 15 min
★ Easy ☆ Cheap

FILLET OF VENISON WITH MUSTARD SAUCE

60 gm unsalted butter
12 × 90 gm fillets of venison (or beef)
60 gm old-style mustard with seeds
(Moutarde a l'ancienne)
1 medium cleaned onion finely chopped
90 ml dry white wine
90 ml beef stock
120 ml fresh double cream

4 servings

Heat the butter in a pan on a moderate heat. Season the fillets and cook to the desired degree of doneness. Remove from the pan, and keep warm. Add the mustard and the onion to the pan. Gently cook for about 1 minute, stirring constantly. Pour in the wine and the stock. Simmer to reduce the level by two-thirds. Add the cream and cook until the sauce begins to thicken. Season to taste. Pour the sauce on to the plate and place the fillets on top, or pour the sauce over the fillets.

Preparation : 15 min • Cooking : 25 min
★ Easy   ☆ Expensive

Bottom left: Fillet of Venison with Mustard Sauce
Bottom right: Escalope de Dinde Alicia
Opposite: Chicken Daube (p. 82)

ESCALOPE DE DINDE ALICIA

1 egg lightly beaten
50 gm plain flour
100 gm white breadcrumbs
2 slices of gruyere cheese
2 slices of cooked ham
4 thin slices of raw turkey breast
60 gm unsalted butter
juice of 1 lemon

2 servings

Place the egg, flour and breadcrumbs into separate containers. Place a slice of cheese and ham on 2 slices of the turkey. Wet the edges of the turkey with a little of the egg.

Place the remaining slices of turkey on top to cover the cheese and ham. Press down the edges of the turkey. Season. Dip the turkey into the flour, then into the egg and cover with breadcrumbs.

Heat the oil in the pan over a moderate heat. Cook the escalopes on each side for 5 minutes. The escalopes should be a light golden brown colour. Remove from the pan. Add the butter to the pan and cook for 1 minute until a very light brown. Add the lemon juice.

Place the escalopes onto a platter and pour the butter mixture over them.

Preparation : 15 min • Cooking : 15 min
★ Easy   ☆ Moderate

CHICKEN DAUBE

1 kilo whole chicken
oil for frying
1 large chopped onion
2 cloves crushed garlic
15 gm fresh coriander leaves
1 cup red wine
15 gm chopped parsley
5 crushed cloves
1 sprig fresh thyme
5 gm crushed root ginger
3 medium chillies cut into four and seeded
500 gm whole peeled tomatoes
seasoning

4 servings

Cut the chicken into bite-sized pieces. Place oil in pan and heat. Cook the chicken pieces in the oil for 5 minutes. Remove from the pan when cooked then set aside and keep warm.

Fry the onions and garlic for 30 seconds in the pan. Add the rest of the ingredients, except the tomatoes, and cook for 1 minute. Cut each of the tomatoes into four and add to the above. Simmer for 5 minutes. Add the chicken to the rest of the mixture. Cook for a further 3 minutes, adding chicken stock if required.

The daube should be a red colour with a rich sauce. Remove the coriander and thyme before serving.

Serve with Creole Rice, Black Lentils and a Vegetable Achard.

Note: Calamary or octopus may be used instead of the chicken. They must be pre-cooked in boiling water.

Preparation : 25 min • Cooking : 15 min
★ Easy ☆ Moderate

BROCHETTE OF CHICKEN

500 gm chicken meat
125 ml olive oil
2 large finely chopped onions
2 crushed cloves of garlic
1 lemon squeezed for juice
10 leaves of fresh coriander
125 ml white wine

4 servings

Cut the chicken into bite-sized pieces. Mix the rest of the ingredients well together. Place the chicken into the mixture, marinate in the refrigerator for 24 hours.

Place the meat onto brochette sticks or skewers. Cook under the grill, turning all the time, or cook on a barbeque with a gentle heat, again turning all the time.

Preparation : 10 min • Cooking : 8 min
★ Easy ☆ Cheap

RABBIT WITH PRUNES

1 rabbit cleaned
100 gm prunes with stones removed
15 ml olive oil
10 gm plain flour
15 gm unsalted butter
220 ml red wine
300 ml chicken stock
1 clove crushed garlic
1 bouquet garni
100 gm cleaned button mushrooms
60 gm cleaned button onions
30 gm bacon cut into lardons
3 gm chopped parsley

3 servings

For the marinade
150 ml red wine
1 large cleaned onion coarsely chopped
1 large cleaned carrot coarsely chopped
6 crushed black peppercorns
1 bouquet garni
30 ml olive oil

Cut the rabbit into six or seven pieces.

Place all of the marinade ingredients into a stainless steel bowl.

Place the pieces of rabbit into the marinade and turn the pieces around in the marinade. Cover the bowl and leave at room temperature for about 10 hours.

Pour boiling water over the prunes and allow to soak for 2 hours.

Drain the rabbit keeping the marinade.

Heat the olive oil and butter in a pan on a low heat. Brown the pieces of rabbit in the pan. Remove from the pan and keep warm.

Into the pan fry gently the carrots and the onions from the marinade.

Sprinkle the flour over the vegetables. Cook and stir until the flour is brown.

Stir in the marinade and the red wine, bringing to the boil. Add the stock, garlic, and the bouquet garni. Replace the pieces of rabbit. Cover the pot and allow to simmer for 25 minutes.

Transfer the rabbit to a shallow casserole. Pass the sauce through a sieve and over the rabbit.

Press down hard so that the vegetables are quite dry.

Fry the bacon; mushrooms and button onions in a pan with a little oil; for about two minutes. Add to the rabbit and mix into the sauce.

Strain the prunes and also add these to the sauce. Cover the casserole with a lid and simmer gently for 10 to 15 minutes.

Remove the rabbit from sauce and keep warm.

Reduce the sauce by ⅓ to enrichen.

Season to taste and add the chopped parsley.

Pour the sauce over the rabbit and serve.

Preparation : 40 min • Cooking : 50 min
★ Difficult ☆ Moderate

CIVET OF HARE

3 cloves garlic
10 gm root ginger
250 gm tomato flesh, no seeds or skin
1 cinnamon stick
6 cloves
1 medium finely chopped onion
10 gm crushed black pepper
1 sprig fresh thyme
15 gm parsley
2 kilos hare (or rabbit) cut into pieces
2 wine glasses dry white wine
oil
seasoning
6 servings

Crush the garlic and ginger together with a little oil. Add the tomato flesh and crush with the above to a fine paste.

Crush the cinnamon stick and cloves with a little water to form a paste.

Add all of the above together and mix with the finely chopped onions. Mix well in a bowl adding the oil and seasoning and a cup of water to make a sauce. Add the thyme and parsley.

Place the hare into the sauce. Marinate for 24 hours in the refrigerator.

Preheat the oven to medium.

After removing the bowl from the refrigerator, place contents into a roasting pan.

Place in the oven for 1 hour. After ½ hour pour over the white wine and crushed black pepper. Mix in and continue cooking until done.

Preparation : 25 min • Cooking : 1 h
★ Easy ☆ Moderate

A QUARTET

OF CUISINES

Mauritius has been very fortunate indeed to have had the influence of the three greatest cuisines ever, with the added bonus of Creole cooking. Culinary forces which, taken individually, oppose each other in taste and flavour. However, just as in a giant jigsaw puzzle, everything seems eventually to fall into place in Mauritian kitchens, with each community borrowing unashamedly from, and enhancing, each other's cuisine.

There are several independent restaurants in Mauritius which specialize in one particular aspect of Mauritian cuisine. In the capital, Port Louis, one finds the Indian influence predominant in *La Bonne Marmite* and in *The Carri Poullé*, the latter named after a plant of Indian origin, a few leaves of which added to the massala during the cooking, give such a typical flavour to the curry.

The former has recently been restored and remodelled by the famous local architect, Maurice Giraud, whose best work has been *Le Touessrok Sun* Hotel and its Ile Aux Cerfs subsidiary, situated at Trou d'Eau Douce on the east coast. *La Bonne Marmite* specializes in Tandoori chicken, served with delicious Nan bread, both cooked the traditional way in a Tandoori oven. *The Carri Poullé*, situated closer to the harbour area, serves a tasty *briani* made with chicken, beef — or, even better, with goat — added to which is a superb selection of tasty chutneys and classic accompaniments.

Since the Chinese community chose Port Louis as the centre of their trading activities, one expects to find a Chinatown area full of the characteristic hustle and bustle — and one is not disappointed. The focal point of Chinatown is, in fact, the Chinese equivalent of the Casino, known as *L'Amicale de Port Louis*, often used as a location for film making, with such stars as Catherine Deneuve, Princess Stéphanie of Monaco and Jean Louis Trintignant. Opposite *l'Amicale* is *Lai Min*, a well-known restaurant of long standing, which pioneered locally adapted Chinese food in Mauritius.

Peter Ngok, born in Hong Kong, decided to make Mauritius his home some five years ago and, in the process, has established the renowned *Canard Laqué* restaurant at *La Pirogue Sun*, with a second branch at *Le Touessrok Sun*. As the name suggests, the *Canard Laqué* is the speciality of the house, and there you will find crisp Peking duck, mixed with a plum sauce, cucumber and spring onions rolled together in a wheat-flour pancake. It is when serving the duck that Peter really

comes into his own, carving his creation with the born showmanship of a successful entertainer.

In Curepipe one finds the accent definitely on French cuisine. There two restaurants really stand out: *La Potinière* and *Le Gourmet*. At *La Potinière* one can find the finest *soufflé de camarons* and palm hearts, served with a slightly spiced *sauce rouge* (red sauce), perfected throughout the island.

Jacqueline Dalais has long been a favourite chef with knowledgeable Mauritians, several of whom, when you talk to them, become glassy-eyed on remembering the succulent seafood Jacqueline prepared years ago at the modest restaurant, once a colonial bungalow, forerunner to the *Touessrok Sun Hotel*. Her restaurant, *Le Gourmet*, recently found a splendid home in a roomy, wooden colonial house with a model of the Eiffel Tower in the garden.

Off the eastern coast, near Trou d'Eau Douce and *Le Touessrok Sun*, one comes across the dream islet of Ile Aux Cerfs, divided by a 10 metre channel from Ilot Mangénie. At low tide, the enormous white sandbank becomes exposed, providing a superb view from the *Chaumière* restaurant, one of the very few restaurants serving authentic Creole and Indian-inspired cuisine.

A six-year stay in Singapore gave French chef Bernard Gouerec a taste of multi-cultural island life, before he took up the reins of the *Touessrok Sun* as Executive Chef. Originally from Brittany, Bernard is no stranger to cooking fish and shellfish. Using modern French cooking methods and techniques, Bernard is combining local ingredients with local culinary influences. The result is delicious.

Barry Andrews, co-author of this book, and his protégé, chef Mesh Boyjonauth, are producing daily a gastronomical feast for guests at the *Saint Géran Sun*. Outdoor barbecues are a regular feature, displaying artistic creations in ice and margarine, and featuring tables laden with salads, hors d'oeuvres and desserts.

Often referred to as the Father of the Nation, Sir Seewoosagur Ramgoolam was Mauritius' first-ever Prime Minister and when he sadly passed away at the end of 1985, he was Governor-General. He was a born statesman, fostered peace and harmony amongst his multi-racial people, provided a sound foundation for the economy and built a democratic country. No wonder, then, that one of the recipes in this chapter is named in his memory.

DELICIOUS DUCK WITH MANGO

1, 2 kg cleaned duck
oil
1 medium peeled onion, finely chopped
1 medium peeled carrot, finely chopped
100 gm castor sugar
60 ml wine vinegar
4 small peeled mangoes
90 gm unsalted butter
2 tots dark rum
60 gm brown sugar, seasoning
4 whole chestnuts

4 servings

Pre-heat the oven to moderate.

Season the duck and brush with little oil. Allow to cook for about 45 minutes.

When cooked, but still pink, remove from the oven. Take the duck out of the tray, and skim off any excess oil. Fry the onion and carrot in a little oil. Remove.

Caramelise the castor sugar in the same pan. Pour on top the wine vinegar and cook for 2 minutes. Add carrots, onion, sugar, vinegar mixture to the duck residue with 2 cups of water. Reduce by two thirds.

Cut the mangoes in half. Puree 4 halves of the mangoes with a little water.

Heat 60 gm of butter in a pan. Cook the mangoes in the butter with the rum and the brown sugar for 1 minute either side. When cooked but still firm, remove from the pan and keep warm.

Add the mango residue to the duck sauce and pour the mango puree into the sauce. Cook again for 2 minutes and strain.

Replace on a low heat and whisk in the remaining 30 gm of the softened butter. Season to taste.

Cut the duck into 4 pieces and place onto serving plate. Pour over the sauce and place ½ a mango by the side.

Decorate with the whole chestnuts.

Preparation : 20 min • Cooking : 1 h 40 min
★ Difficult ☆ Moderate

FILLETS OF BEEF WITH THREE PEPPERS

125 gm unsalted butter
8 × 90 gm fillet steaks
1 small onion, finely chopped
250 ml dry red wine
5 gm fresh green peppercorns
5 gm fresh black peppercorns
5 gm fresh pink peppercorns
250 ml beef stock
60 ml double cream
salt to taste

4 servings

Heat 30 gm of the butter in a pan.

Season the fillets and fry to the desired degree. Remove from the pan, put aside and keep warm.

Fry the onions in the pan until soft but not brown. Pour in the red wine.

Take a pinch from each of the peppercorns and set aside for garnish. Add the remaining peppercorns to the wine and reduce the liquor to one third.

Pour in the beef stock and again reduce to about half of the volume. Remove the pan from the heat and whisk in the remaining softened butter and the cream.

Season to taste.

Pour the sauce through a strainer. Place the warm steaks on the plates and pour over the sauce. Sprinkle the peppercorns that were set aside on top.

Preparation : 15 min • Cooking : 20 min
★ Easy ☆ Moderate

Previous page: Roasted Pork Loin with Honey (p. 101)
Top: Fillets of Beef with Three Peppers
Bottom: Delicious Duck with Mango

RABBIT A LA MAURICIENNE

250 gm soaked prunes
1 large cleaned rabbit
3 cups red wine
50 gm pork fat
oil for frying
2 onions, chopped
1 bay leaf
5 gm rosemary
5 crushed cloves
5 gm coriander
1 tsp cornflour dissolved in a little water
2 tots dark rum
seasoning

4 servings

Remove the stones from the prunes.

Cut the rabbit into bite-sized pieces, marinate for 24 hours in the red wine.

Cut the pork fat into small dice.

Place the oil in a casserole to heat and fry the onions until soft. Add the rest of the ingredients, except the prunes and rum. Cook for 1 minute.

Remove the rabbit from the wine and put into the casserole. Cook for 2 minutes turning all the time. Season.

Add the red wine and water, sufficient to cover. Allow to cook for 40 minutes on a low heat.

Add the prunes and rum 10 minutes before serving.

Season to taste.

Preparation : 25 min • Cooking 55 min
★ Easy   ☆ Cheap

FRICASSEE OF FRESH RABBIT WITH CURRY SAUCE

4 saddles of rabbit off the bone
500 ml rabbit stock, seasoned
2 tblsp Curry Sauce
250 ml Hollandaise Sauce
1 pineapple cleaned
and cut into batons

4 servings

Roll the saddles up and tie with some string.

Pre-heat the oven to 220°F (110°C).

Bring the rabbit stock to the boil in a pan. Place the saddles into the stock and put into the oven for approximately 10 minutes, then check to see if the meat is cooked.

Heat the curry sauce and strain then add slowly to the hollandaise, whisking well all the time.

Remove the rabbit from the stock after it is cooked. Dry with a clean cloth, and cut off the string.

Place the rabbit onto a plate, cover with the prepared curry sauce and decorate with pineapple cut into batons.

Serve with white rice.

Note: Care must be taken when mixing the curry sauce into the hollandaise otherwise it may separate.

Preparation : 35 min • Cooking : 25 min
★ Easy   ☆ Cheap

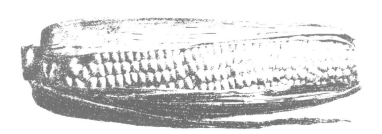

QUAIL EGG BROCHETTES

For the meat balls:
260 gm boneless chicken meat
2 egg whites
oil for frying
10 gm sugar
3 tsp soya sauce
1 tot dry sherry
1 orange squeezed for the juice
12 servings

For the brochettes
1 medium cucumber
2 tsp malt vinegar
12 quail eggs
12 very small tomatoes

For the meat balls:

Cook and finely mince the chicken meat, season to taste. Mix the meat and the egg whites together to form a paste. Form the meat into 24 meat balls.

Heat oil about 2.5 cm deep in the pan. Fry the meat balls in the oil until golden brown. Remove from the oil and drain.

Place the sugar, soya, sherry and orange juice in a pan. Stir on a low heat until the sugar dissolves.

Place the meat balls in the sauce and turn them over constantly. Simmer gently until the sauce forms a glaze over the meatballs. Remove from heat, cool.

For the brochettes:

Peel and remove the seeds from the cucumber. Cut into 4 cm square cubes. Marinate in vinegar, salt for 10 min.

Boil the eggs for 3 minutes until hard, cool and remove the shell.

Thread onto each skewer one meat ball, a piece of cucumber, one egg, one tomato and another meatball.

Cook on the barbeque for 4 minutes.

Serve hot with rice.

Note: More sauce may be made and served over the brochettes.

Preparation : 25 min • Cooking 15 min
★ Easy   ☆ Moderate

RED SWEET PEPPERS WITH EGG

4 large red sweet peppers
450 gm fresh mushrooms finely chopped
1 large onion finely chopped
1 tot port
1 clove crushed garlic
30 gm unsalted butter
4 small eggs
1 pinch rosemary
seasoning

4 servings

Pre-heat the oven to about 400° F (200° C).

Place the peppers under the grill until the skin begins to blacken.

Peel off the skin of the peppers leaving them whole.

Cut off the top and remove the seeds from inside.

Heat the butter in a pan on a low heat.

Add the onions and cook until transparent.

Add the mushrooms and the port and stir fry for about 5 minutes.

Replace the lid on top of the four sweet peppers.

Bake in the oven for about 15 minutes. Serve hot.

Preparation : 20 min • Cooking : 25 min
★ Very easy   ☆ Cheap

91

SWEET AND SOUR PORK

500 gm lean pork cut into bite-sized pieces
60 ml dark soya sauce
30 ml dry sherry
15 gm finely grated root ginger
120 gm cornflour
1 small onion, coarsely chopped
1 large tomato cut into bite-sized pieces
1 stick celery sliced into bite-sized pieces
1 large thinly sliced carrot
1 green capsicum, cleaned,
sliced into bite-sized pieces
1 red capsicum, cleaned,
sliced into bite-sized pieces
½ small pineapple, cleaned,
sliced into bite-sized pieces
2 cloves crushed garlic
30 gm tomato puree
90 gm sugar
90 gm chicken stock
30 gm cornflour
60 ml white or malt vinegar

4 servings

Marinate the pork in the soya, sherry and the ginger for 30 minutes. Heat the oil in a pan to very hot. Roll the pork pieces into the cornflour. Shake off any excess. Deep fry until a golden brown and allow to drain then set aside and keep warm. Heat a little oil in another pan. Add all the vegetables plus the garlic and stir fry for 1 minute. Add the tomato puree, sugar and stock. Sir in and mix well. Blend the cornflour with the vinegar. Pour into the vegetables to thicken. Return the pork to the vegetables and cook for 1 more minute. Season to taste. Serve with Cantonese rice.

Preparation : 35 min • Cooking : 10 min
★ Very easy ☆ Cheap

Opposite, top left: Mutton Briani (p. 100), top right:
Beef Rougaille (p. 100)
Bottom: Mauritian Pot au Feu
Right: Sweet and Sour Pork

MAURITIAN POT AU FEU

2 chicken breasts
5 litres chicken stock
500 gm ox tail
500 gm topside of beef
12 white peppercorns
8 button onions, 4 carrots
4 celery sticks, 8 small turnips
1 small cabbage heart
1 fresh chilli, seeded, crushed
4 leeks, 4 small potatoes
1 sprig thyme, 4 cloves
4 cloves crushed garlic
1 lemon squeezed for the juice

4 servings

De-bone breasts. Bring stock to the boil, add oxtail and beef, salt and peppercorns. Simmer for 2½ hours.

Clean vegetables. Cut the carrots, celery and turnips to 5 cm lengths. Leave cabbage whole.

Place all the vegetables into the casserole. Add the thyme, garlic, cloves and the chicken. Cook for 20 minutes.

Cut the beef into slices, and the chicken breast into two. Cut cabbage into 4.

Serve in a clean casserole and stir in the lemon juice.

Preparation : 30 min • Cooking : 3 h
★ Difficult ☆ Moderate

ISLAND RAGOUT

750 gm topside
1 tsp peanut oil
24 cleaned button onions
6 medium diced peeled potatoes
3 large sliced peeled carrots
3 large chopped peeled tomatoes
120 gm smoked fish
1 pinch ground cinnamon
1 bay leaf
3 tsp peanut chutney
1 large crushed chilli
1 tsp malt vinegar
seasoning

6 servings

Cut the meat into bite-sized pieces.

Place the oil in a pan and heat. Fry the onions until soft and then add the meat. Cook for 5 minutes stirring all the time.

Add the vegetables to the meat and cook for a further 5 minutes. Pour in two glasses of water and stir continuously. Cook on a low heat for 25 minutes with a lid on the pan, add more liquid if necessary.

Crush the fish to a puree and add to the meat then add the rest of the ingredients and fold in. Cover with the lid again and cook for a further 10 minutes.

Serve hot with Creole Rice.

Preparation : 25 min • Cooking : 45 min
★ Easy ☆ Cheap

STUFFED PAWPAW

1 green pawpaw, medium size
vegetable oil for frying
20 gm finely chopped onions
3 cloves crushed garlic
5 gm crushed root ginger
½ kilo minced beef
6 large chopped tomatoes
3 small crushed red chillies
3 gm crushed black peppercorns
200 gm white breadcrumbs
60 gm grated cheddar cheese
5 gm salt

6 servings

Cut the pawpaw in half lengthways and remove the seeds.

Heat the oil in a pan. Pre-heat the oven to moderate, 350°F (180°C).

Place the onions, garlic and the ginger in the oil.

Sir fry for 1 minute, do not allow to colour.

Add the beef and stir. Cook for 3 minutes.

Add the tomatoes, chillies, salt and pepper.

Stir well and cook for a further 2 minutes on a fast heat.

When the mixture has cooked, pour into the pawpaw shells. Place the shells in a roasting tin. Pour water into the tin to the depth of 2.5 cm up the sides of the pawpaw.

Place in the oven and bake for 1 hour, covering with foil if necessary.

Combine the cheese and breadcrumbs.

Remove the pawpaw from the oven and sprinkle the cheese mixture over the top.

Bake again for 10 minutes. The pawpaw should be soft and the top delicately brown.

Serve hot with Creole Sauce served separately.

Preparation : 25 min • Cooking 30 min
★ Easy ☆ Cheap

SPRING VEGETABLES WITH BEEF

250 gm stewing beef
40 gm cleaned French beans
oil for frying
40 gm cleaned sliced onions
3 cloves crushed garlic
2 small crushed fresh chillies
40 gm cleaned batons of carrots
40 gm cleaned diced cabbage
40 gm cauliflower pieces
40 gm peeled diced turnip
40 gm peeled diced potatoes
40 gm mange-tout
40 gm broccoli pieces
2 litres beef stock
1 sprig fresh thyme
seasoning

4 servings

Cut the beef into bite size pieces.

Cut the French beans into 2 cm pieces.

Heat the oil in a pan on a low heat and cook the onions. Do not allow to colour. Stir the garlic and the chillies into the onions. Add the beef and cook for 5 minutes.

Put all of the prepared vegetables into the pot. With a wooden spoon, stir the meat into the vegetables. Pour over enough beef stock to cover the ingredients, add the thyme. Place the lid on to the pan and cook. When vegetables and meat are tender remove from heat.

Serve with rice and Tomato Chutney.

Preparation : 25 min • Cooking : 40 min
★ Very easy   ☆ Cheap

FILLET STEAK ISLE DE FRANCE

oil for frying
3 × 180 fillet steaks, trimmed to desired
size
1 large finely chopped onion
1 cup dry white wine
10 gm tomato puree
1 cup beef stock
1 tsp horseradish
90 ml cream
2 tot Drambuie
20 gm unsalted butter
1 bay leaf

3 servings

Heat the oil in a pan on a moderate heat. Cook the fillets in a pan to the desired degree. Remove from the pan, put to one side and keep warm.

Add the finely chopped onions into the same pan. Cook for 1 minute but do not allow to colour. Pour in the white wine and cook for 2 minutes stirring well, reduce by half. Stir in the tomato puree and the beef stock. Add the bay leaf. Cook until it has reduced to ⅔ of its original volume and is a smooth sauce. Add the horseradish and the cream. Stir into the sauce. Cook for 1 minute

Pour in the Drambuie and whisk in the softened butter at the last moment. Take off the heat.

Serve the fillets with the sauce immediately.

Preparation : 20 min • Cooking : 10 min
★ Very easy   ☆ Moderate

SIRLOIN STEAK MALAGASSE

oil for frying
1 large finely chopped onion
10 gm crushed black peppercorns
1 clove crushed garlic
10 gm green peppercorns
1 bay leaf, 1 cup red wine
2 cups beef stock
1 tsp red currant jelly, 60 gm cream
5 gm chopped fresh basil leaves
3 medium sirloin steaks
½ cleaned and chopped pineapple

3 servings

Heat the oil in a pan. Add the chopped onions and cook for 1 minute.

Stir in the crushed peppercorns, garlic, green peppercorns, bay leaf and the red wine. Cook for a further minute, stirring with a wooden spoon. Pour in stock, red currant jelly and stir. Reduce by half.

Stir in the cream, and cook for 2 minutes. Season, add the basil.

Cook the sirloin steaks in a separate pan; place onto a heated platter. Add to the sauce any juice left from cooking the steaks, mixing it in well.

Pour the sauce over the steaks and place the chopped pineapple on the top.

Preparation : 15 min • Cooking : 15 min
★ Very easy   ☆ Moderate

BEEF WITH SESAME SEEDS

350 gm sirloin of beef trimmed of all fat
1 orange
30 ml rice wine
oil for deep frying
10 ml sesame oil
60 gm brown sugar
15 gm sesame seeds

4 servings

Cut the beef into thin slices.

Grate the orange very finely. Squeeze the orange and mix with the zest and the rice wine.

Heat the oil until very hot. Fry a small quantity of the beef in the oil for 20 seconds and allow to drain. Repeat this process twice with the rest of the beef.

In a wok heat the sesame oil and the sugar. Allow the sugar to begin to caramelise. Very quickly pour in the orange juice mixture and the sesame seeds. Stir very quickly, then add the beef immediately. Mix everything together and remove from the fire onto a serving dish.

From the moment the sugar starts to caramelise the remaining operation should take less than 1 minute.

Serve with Cantonese rice.

Preparation : 20 min • Cooking : 5 min
★ Difficult   ☆ Moderate

DAUBE OF GOAT

90 ml water
15 ml oil
1 kilo goat meat (or lamb)
cut into bite-sized pieces
3 sprigs fresh thyme
(or ¼ level tsp dried)
3 elaichi (cardamom) seeds
1 medium crushed onion
2 cloves crushed garlic
10 gm crushed root ginger
10 gm powdered cummin
10 gm red chilli powder
5 gm powdered turmeric
500 gm crushed tomato flesh,
no skin or seeds
150 gm peeled potato
150 gm garden peas
15 gm chopped coriander leaves
10 gm salt

5 servings

Bring the water and the oil to the boil together. Cook the goat, thyme and the elaichi (cardamom) seeds until all the water is absorbed. Add the onions, spices and the tomatoes. Stir in until well mixed, cooking all of the time. Pour in a cup of water and the salt.

Cut the potato into dice and fry until half cooked. Cook until the goat is tender.

Add the potatoes and the peas and cook for a further five minutes.

Sprinkle with chopped coriander and Tomato Chutney.

Serve with Delicious Rice.

Preparation : 15 min • Cooking : 30 min
★ Very easy   ☆ Moderate

GRILLED MINCED LAMB BROCHETTES

250 gm lean minced lamb
4 cleaned spring onions
1 large cleaned carrot
1 large cleaned chilli
5 basil leaves, finely chopped
5 gm fresh rosemary,
finely chopped
60 gm fresh parsley,
finely chopped
2 cloves crushed garlic
5 gm crushed root ginger
60 gm plain yoghurt
1 large egg
Lea and Perrins sauce
seasoning

4 servings

Place all the items together and mince very finely. Roll into the shape of a cigar. Push onto skewers, patting the meat so it retains its shape round the skewers.

Refrigerate for 30 minutes so that the meat firms a little.

Cook on the barbeque or under a grill turning from time to time so that the meat browns evenly. Serve with Creole Sauce and with plain white rice or Delicious Rice.

Preparation : 15 min • Cooking : 10 min
★ Very easy   ☆ Cheap

Opposite left: Sirloin Steak Malagasse
Opposite right: Beef with Sesame Seeds

STUFFED PATTISON

4 medium pattisons (gem squash)
olive oil
1 medium onion, finely chopped
2 cloves crushed garlic
10 gm crushed root ginger
½ kilo minced lean beef
2 large chopped red tomatoes
1 medium crushed chilli
10 finely crushed black peppercorns
5 gm thyme finely chopped
60 gm grated cheddar cheese
60 gm white breadcrumbs
Creole Sauce
seasoning

4 servings

Cut the tops off of the pattisons and remove the seeds with a spoon.

Heat the oil in a pan. Pre-heat the oven to 300°F (160°C).

Place the onion, garlic and ginger in the oil. Stir fry for 1 minute, but do not allow to colour. Add the beef, and stir for 3 minutes.

Stir in the tomatoes, chillies, pepper and thyme. Stir well and cook for a further 2 minutes.

Spoon the mixture into the pattison and replace the lid on top.

Pour water into a tin 2.5 cm up the sides of the pattison. Cook in the oven for 20 minutes, covering with foil.

Remove pattison from the oven and take the top off. Sprinkle with the cheese and the breadcrumbs combined.

Grill until golden brown. The pattison should be soft to touch but still firm.

After grilling, replace the top halfway on, place heated Creole Sauce in the liquidiser and blend for one minute.

Pour the sauce on the plate and place the pattison on top of the sauce.

Preparation : 20 min • Cooking : 30 min
★ Easy ☆ Cheap

RAGOUT OF GOAT

1 leg young goat (or 2 kg leg of lamb)
2 medium onions
4 large tomatoes
1 large chou chou
olive oil
1 glass red wine
2 cups water
1 clove crushed garlic
10 gm fresh thyme
10 gm crushed root ginger
15 gm curry powder
seasoning

4 servings

Cut the goat meat into bite-sized pieces.

Clean and chop the onions very finely, cut the tomatoes into 6 pieces each, clean and cut the chou chou into pieces.

Place the oil into a pan and heat.

Season the goat with salt and pepper, place into the oil and cook for 5 minutes. Remove from the oil.

Cook the onions in the same pan, adding the red wine. Add the rest of the ingredients then the goat leg and cook slowly until the meat is tender. Season to taste.

Serve with Creole Rice.

Note: If you prefer a less 'gamey' flavour, soak the meat in milk for 6 hours or more, in the refrigerator.

Preparation : 15 min • Cooking : 25 min
★ Easy ☆ Moderate

Opposite: Stuffed Pattison

98

BEEF ROUGAILLE

750 gm topside
oil for frying
750 gm fresh tomatoes
4 large chillies cut lengthways
8 chopped spring onions
3 large sliced onions
15 gm grated root ginger
1 sprig fresh thyme
3 cloves crushed garlic
5 gm chopped parsley
15 fresh coriander leaves

6 servings

Cut the topside into bite-sized cubes and season.

Heat the oil in a pan, add the topside and cook for 4 minutes. Remove the meat from the oil and set aside, keeping warm.

Cut the tomatoes into quarters and clean the chillies. In the pan cook gently 4 of the chopped spring onions for 1 minute.

Add the onions, ginger, thyme, garlic, chillies and the parsley to the oil. Fry gently on a medium heat for 2 minutes.

Add the tomatoes and stir in. Cook for a further 4 minutes.

Add the beef, stir well and simmer for 10 minutes. Season to taste. Add the rest of the spring onions. Chop the coriander leaves and add half to the mixture.

When about to serve, sprinkle the rest of the coriander on top.

Serve with Creole Rice and Mixed Vegetable Achard.

Preparation : 15 min • Cooking : 20 min
★ Very easy   ☆ Cheap

MUTTON BRIANI

1¼ kilo lean mutton pieces
cut into bite-sized pieces
20 gm crushed root ginger
20 gm crushed garlic
1 cinnamon stick
4 cloves
15 gm powdered coriander
4 elaichi (cardamom seeds)
30 gm salt
500 gm basmati rice
200 gm lentils
2 large onions sliced and fried
500 gm crushed tomato flesh,
skinned and seeded
30 gm plain yoghurt
5 gm red chilli powder
250 gm peeled potatoes
cut into bite-sized pieces
24 leaves fresh mint, finely chopped
6 hard boiled eggs, shelled
10 gm green chilli powder
200 gm unsalted butter
10 gm turmeric
2 medium onions crushed
24 leaves fresh coriander finely chopped
20 gm salt

6 servings

Mix the mutton pieces with the crushed ginger, garlic and 20 gm of salt. Allow to marinate for 2 hours.

Bring to the boil ½ litre of water adding the cinnamon, cloves, elaichi and 30 gm salt.

Rinse and clean the basmati rice. Add to the boiling water and allow to cook uncovered. When the rice is half cooked, drain and keep warm.

Cook the lentils in salted water, until well cooked but still firm.

Pre-heat the oven to moderate.

In a large casserole, put the pieces of marinated mutton with the fried onions, crushed onions, tomatoes, yoghurt, all the spices and add 1¾ cups of cold water. Mix all these ingredients well together.

Brown the potato in a little oil.

Fry the boiled eggs in a little oil for 3 minutes turning all the time.

Melt the butter and mix it into the above mixture of spices and mutton.

Sprinkle the lentils all over the mixture. Place the potatoes on top of the lentils. Pour over the rice to cover the complete mixture.

Place a close-fitting lid on the casserole dish and cook in the oven for 45 minutes.

Preparation : 2 h 35 min • Cooking : 1 h 15 min
★ Difficult   ☆ Moderate

B.B.Q. SPARE RIBS

600 gm pork spareribs
15 gm curry powder
crushed garlic
10 gm five spice powder
60 ml soya sauce
15 gm salt
5 gm monosodium glutamate (optional)
30 gm sugar
30 ml rice wine
5 gm crushed black pepper
30 ml honey

6 servings

Cut the spare ribs into the required portion size.

Mix the rest of the ingredients together. Place the spare ribs into the mixture, coating each portion well and marinate for 6 hours.

Remove from the marinade and cook on a gentle barbeque with no flame, or in a very hot oven.

Or coat the spare ribs with cornflour and fry in oil in a pan.

Preparation : 10 min • Cooking 10 min
★ Easy   ☆ Moderate

ROASTED PORK LOIN WITH HONEY

2 kilo lean pork loin
60 gm soft honey
180 gm brown sugar
2 tots dark rum
100 ml dark soya sauce
15 gm finely grated root ginger
1 clove crushed garlic
1 pinch ground black pepper
1 lime squeezed for juice
30 gm cornflour dissolved in a little water
500 ml chicken stock

8 servings

Lightly score the pork loin diagonally 1 cm deep by about 2.5 cm apart on the fat side.

Mix the honey, sugar, rum and soya sauce together. Place the pork into the mixture, scored side down. Marinate covered for 12 hours in the refrigerator.

Pre-heat the oven to 300°F (160°C) Turn the pork over and cook in the oven in the same mixture. Cook for approximately 1½ hours.

Remove the pork from the pan when cooked and keep warm.

Put the pan on the heat and add the remainder of the ingredients to the remaining residue, skim off any excess fat. Bring to the boil, stirring constantly. Season to taste.

Slice the pork and serve the sauce around the edges.

Preparation : 20 min • Cooking : 10 min
★ Easy   ☆ Moderate

NUT OF LAMB
A LA MARIE-FRANCE

2 large onions
250 gm fresh mushrooms
30 gm unsalted butter
1 clove crushed garlic
3 small tomatoes peeled
and seeded
2 tots port
1 medium loin of lamb trimmed
and boned
olive oil for frying
3 chicken livers
2 cups dry red wine

10 gm tomato puree
3 cups beef stock
1 bay leaf
3 gm rosemary
1 cup Bearnaise Sauce
seasoning

6 servings

Chop one onion and the mushrooms separately into a very fine dice.

Melt the butter in a pan. Add the onion and garlic to the butter and cook for 1 minute. Do not allow to colour.

Stir in the diced mushrooms and cook for a further minute. Pour in the port. Season to taste and cook until the mix-

ture is quite dry.

Remove from the heat and allow to cool.

Lay the loin flat on the table and season. Spoon the mushroom mix along the centre lengthways so that it forms a filling.

Roll the loin up and tie with string to keep it in shape.

Refrigerate for 30 minutes to make the meat firm. This makes cutting easier.

Cut the loin into 2.5 cm pieces, ensuring that the string holds the shape of each slice so that you have even servings of the lamb surrounding the savoury filling.

Place the oil in a pan and heat. Cook the lamb in the oil for 5 minutes. Turn and cook for further five minutes.

Remove from the pan and put to one side, keeping warm.

Chop the chicken livers into a fine dice. Finely chop the remaining onion.

Drop it in the oil and cook for 1 minute. Do not allow to colour. Add the chicken livers and cook for half a minute.

Pour in the red wine and stir well. Add the tomato puree, beef stock, bay leaf and rosemary. Stir well to form a smooth sauce then continue cooking, stirring from time to time until the sauce is reduced by half.

Remove the string from each piece of lamb. Place the hot lamb onto a warm serving dish. Cover with the sauce.

On each piece of lamb place a half of the seeded tomato. Spoon the Bearnaise over the lamb.

Place under a grill to brown lightly.

Serve immediately with vegetables of your choice.

Preparation : 35 min • Cooking 30 min
★ Difficult   ☆ Moderate

Opposite: Nut of Lamb à la Marie-France
Bottom: Island Ragout (p. 98)

FILLET OF LAMB RAMGOOLAM

1 thick slice of aubergine
2 fillets of lamb
60 gm butter
15 gm finely chopped onion
1 clove crushed garlic
10 gm pimento, 30 gm mushrooms,
10 gm green pepper,
all finely chopped
10 gm roasted flaked almonds
5 finely chopped mint leaves
2 tots port, 1 tot brandy
1 glass white wine, 5 gm flour
1 whole peeled tomato
Bearnaise Sauce

2 servings

Sprinkle both sides of the aubergine with a little salt. Take the two fillets of lamb and cut a piece 10 cm from the centre of each fillet. Cut along the length of the fillets so as to flatten them. Place 30 grams of butter in a pan to heat. Add the onions and garlic and cook until soft but not coloured. Add the pimento, mushroom, green pepper, almonds and two of the chopped mint leaves. Cook for 2 minutes, add one tot of port and the brandy. Flame the brandy and stir into the mushroom mix; season to taste.

Take the flattened lamb fillets and season. Spread the mushroom mix along the length of one fillet. Place the other fillet on top to cover completely the mushroom mix. Tie the fillet with string in three places to help keep its shape. Heat 30 gm of butter in a pan. Cook the fillet in the hot butter for 1 minute. Turn continuously. Place the pan with the fillet in a hot oven. Cook for 5 minutes. Heat 15 gm of butter in a pan. Wash the salt off the aubergine and dry well. Cook for 3 minutes in the butter set aside and keep warm. When cooked remove the lamb.

Replace the pan on the heat and add the white wine. There should be a little of the mushroom mix left in the pan from the cooking of the lamb. Mix together the flour and 10 gm of butter to a paste. Stir into the wine, add remaining port, mint. Cook until sauce thickens and season.

Cut tomato in half. Remove seeds.

Cut the fillet into three pieces carefully. Remove the string. Place the three pieces of lamb fillet onto the cooked aubergine. Put the tomato on top, cover with sauce.

Spoon over the top some Bearnaise sauce. Brown under a hot grill.

Serve immediately with vegetables.

Preparation : 20 min. • Cooking : 20 min·
★ Difficult   ☆ Moderate

FILLET OF LAMB LA BOURDONNAIS

1 large green pepper
1 large red pepper
6 trimmed and seasoned fillets of lamb
20 gm paprika
oil for frying
1 large finely chopped onion
60 gm sliced mushrooms
2 wine glasses dry white wine
125 ml thick cream
2 tots calvados

3 servings

Cut the peppers in half and remove the seeds. Cut into a fine julienne.

Roll lamb fillets into the paprika.

Heat the oil in a pan on a moderate heat. Cook the lamb fillets for 2 minutes on each side. Remove and keep warm.

Cook the onion in the oil for 1 minute in the same pan. Do not allow to colour. Add the mushrooms and the sliced peppers. Stir fry for 1 minute.

Pour in the white wine and allow to simmer for 3 minutes. Blend in the thick cream and stir well. Cook for a further 2 minutes, simmer gently. Add the calvados. Season to taste. Pour the sauce over the hot lamb fillets.

Serve with white rice.

Preparation : 20 min • Cooking 10 min
★ Easy   ☆ Moderate

ROAST MARINATED LEG OF LAMB

1 tsp ground cumin
120 gm plain yoghurt
30 gm tamarind paste
olive oil
12 fresh coriander leaves finely chopped
2 tbsps sesame seeds
3 pinch cayenne pepper
1 medium leg of lamb
4 oranges squeezed for juice
1 lemon squeezed for juice
250 ml fresh cream
salt, black pepper

6 servings

Heat a pan on a very low fire. Fry the cumin for just 10 seconds and take off the heat. Add the yoghurt, tamarind, olive oil, coriander, sesame and the cayenne. Stir well to form a paste.

Make several deep incisions into the leg of lamb with a very sharp knife. Spread the yoghurt mixture over the lamb, pressing it into the incisions. Marinate for 12 hours in the refrigerator, covered.

Remove from the refrigerator and leave out for 1 hour.

Preheat the oven for 300°F (160°C). Place the lamb in a tray and into the oven. Cook the lamb for 12 minutes per ½ kilogram of meat. Baste the meat often whilst it is roasting.

10 minutes before it is ready pour over the lamb the orange and lemon juice. When cooked remove from the oven.

Remove the joint from the pan and keep warm. Place the pan onto a low heat with all of the juices, add the cream and bring to the boil for a few minutes, stirring constantly. Season to taste.

Serve as a sauce with the lamb.

Preparation : 20 min • Cooking 30 min
★ Easy   ☆ Moderate

LAMB AND LENTIL STEW

300 gm black lentils
½ tsp fenugreek
75 ml olive oil
2 medium onions, chopped
1 kilo neck of lamb, cut into pieces
90 gm tomato puree
1 tsp Hot Chilli Sauce
2 tsp turmeric
3 cloves crushed garlic
90 gm garden peas
120 gm white haricots beans
soaked for 1 hour
150 gm potatoes, peeled and cut into cubes
12 leaves fresh coriander
12 leaves fresh dill
150 gm macaroni

6 servings

Cook the lentils and fenugreek together until the lentils are quite soft. Cook in a pressure steamer or for 2 hours in gently boiling water. Keep the lid on the pot but stir often to prevent burning. Add more water when necessary.

When the lentil are cooked, strain, keeping the liquor. Set both aside.

Whilst the lentils are cooking, heat the oil in a pan. Cook the onions but do not allow to brown. Add the neck of lamb and fry for 15 minutes on a low heat. Stir in the tomato puree, chilli, turmeric and garlic. Pour in 1 litre water and stir well. Cook for 30 minutes.

Add the peas, white haricots and potatoes. Cook for a further 20 minutes.

If more liquid is required add the lentil water.

Add the coriander, dill and lentils. Add the macaroni and cook for another 10 minutes.

Serve with white rice.

Preparation : 20 min • Cooking : 1 h 30 min
★ Easy   ☆ Moderate

THE SPICES OF
MAURITIUS

The best curries are prepared, not with pre-packaged curry powder, but with a paste that is the result of crushing several spices on a flat, smooth rock known as a *roche carri*. Curiously enough, this is not, as is commonly believed, an Indian invention, but is the distant offshoot of the same stone Alexander the Great carried with him during the Greek invasion of India. The spices used for crushing on the *roche carri* are aniseeds (which should be roasted before), chillis, cinnamon, root ginger, garlic cloves, caraway seeds, coriander seeds, turmeric (sometimes incorrectly called saffron), mustard seeds, black pepper and the fresh leaves known as *carri poullé*.

It is safe to say that Mauritians would starve if they were to be deprived of their chilli, which is placed prominently on the table, as in Europe one would place a pot of mustard alongside the salt and pepper. The chilli is a pepper which is produced in three varieties in Mauritius: *Piment carri*, the least hot and served deep-fried in batter, *ti-piment* (small) and *gros piment* (medium-sized). The small chillies are usually the hottest and even hotter are other small chillies from Rodrigues, an island which is part of Mauritius. But the hottest of them all — still to be found in Mauritius and Rodrigues, but rarely used now — is the squarish-type, *piment cabri* (goat chilli — perhaps because goats like them). They are of the same family as the Mexican variety, and they may burn a hole in your tongue if you are not careful! Indeed, one has to be careful when handling chillies as they contain volatile oils that may be extremely irritating to sensitive skins. If you prefer to serve a milder form of chilli, soak them in cold, salted water for one or two hours.

Rum is frequently used as a fiery flavouring agent in Mauritian dishes and, if liked, you can improve its depth of flavour by marinating whole chillies in ½ a litre of it for a fortnight.

The accompaniments to curries and other Mauritian spicy dishes are extremely important. Chutney or *chatini*, as it is locally termed, is a lightly-pickled fruit or vegetable, which is finely chopped or minced and sometimes flavoured with onion, chilli and other spices. Tomato, coconut, cucumber and peanuts are the most popular. The other principal accompaniment is *achard*, which is a pickled tropical fruit or vegetable which is mixed with oil and mustard seeds and other flavourings. The most common are lemon, mango, palm heart, the poetically-named *fruit de cythère*, and vegetables.

NARAISI KAFTA

Meat balls with egg inside
1 medium onion finely chopped
400 gm finely minced beef
2 cloves crushed garlic
60 gm curry powder
5 gm turmeric
1 medium chilli
cleaned and crushed
1 cup water
50 gm split pea flour
2 large eggs
30 gm natural yoghurt
5 medium hard boiled eggs
60 gm cornflour

5 servings

Place a little oil in a pan on a moderate heat. Cook the onion until soft, add meat, cook for 1 minute. Add the garlic, curry powder, turmeric and chilli. Cook for 1 minute stirring all the time. Pour in the cup of water and bring to the boil. Cook until all the water has been absorbed. Sprinkle the split pea flour on top and stir in. Now cook until the meat is quite soft. Beat and mash the mixture very well.

Lightly beat one egg, whisk into the yoghurt, stir well into the meat.

Remove the shell from the boiled eggs.

Take some of the meat into your hand. Flatten it against the palm.

Place one of the eggs in the centre and fold over the meat, to cover the egg completely. Do this four more times, using all of the mixture. Place the oil for frying on a moderate heat. Beat the remaining eggs with a little salt. Roll the meat ball in the cornflour, dip into the beaten egg and fry in oil until a golden brown.

Drain well and serve hot.

Note: To curry the kaftas, use the curry sauce from the Chicken and Lobster Curry (overleaf) adding a fine julienne of green peppers.

Preparation : 35 min • Cooking : 8 min
★ Difficult　☆ Moderate

CURRIED CHICKEN LIVERS

500 gm chicken livers
50 ml olive oil
1 small onion finely chopped
60 gm dry English mustard
20 gm curry powder
10 gm crushed root ginger
3 cloves garlic, crushed
90 gm garden peas
10 gm fresh coriander leaves
finely chopped
10 gm parsley, chopped
15 gm salt

4 servings

Wash the chicken livers in running cold water. Cut each liver in half.

Heat the oil in a pan. Cook the onions gently but do not brown.

Add the mustard, curry powder, ginger and the garlic. Stir well and cook for 30 seconds.

Add the chicken livers and cook, stirring often.

Cook for about 6 minutes or until livers lose their pinkness.

Add the peas and a little water. Cook for another 3 minutes.

Serve with Creole Rice.

Sprinkle the livers with seasonings, parsley and coriander leaves just before serving.

Preparation : 10 min • Cooking : 12 min
★ Very easy　☆ Cheap

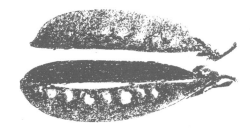

Previous page: Tomato and Coriander Chutney (p. 119)

DHOLL PITA

350 gm dholl (yellow split peas)
1½ litres water
30 gm ghee
2 medium onions, finely chopped
10 gm crushed root ginger
10 curry leaves
3 cloves crushed garlic
3 small red chillies cut into 4
15 gm crushed turmeric
15 gm curry powder
60 gm chopped beef

4 servings

Cook the dholl in the water with the curry leaves until soft.

Melt the ghee in a pan, over a low heat. Place the onions in the ghee but do not brown. Fry spices for 1 minute with onion.

Add the chopped beef and cook for a further 2 minutes. Add the cooked dholl.

Cook for a further 10 minutes adding sufficient water to cover and season to taste. Serve with chopped fresh coriander leaves on top and coconut chutney.

Note: If using black lentils in place of dholl replace curry powder with 150 gm of thinly sliced carrot.

For the pastry:
500 gm flour
pinch salt
15 ml oil
water

Make a firm paste with the ingredients and knead very well.

Take the paste and roll out very thinly. Cut into small squares or fancy shapes.

Drop the pieces into the cooked dholl mixture and cook again gently for about 5 minutes. Care must be taken not to cook the pastry shapes too much — they should be cooked but not soft.

Preparation : 20 min • Cooking : 25 min
★ Easy ☆ Cheap

FRESH PRAWN WITH GINSENG

16 large prawns
2 tots brandy
1 litre boiling water
1 pinch salt
10 ml ginseng liquid

4 servings

Place the prawns in a stainless steel dish. Pour the brandy over them. Toss well in the brandy.

Tip the contents of the bowl into the boiling water. Add the salt. Allow the prawns to boil for 4 minutes.

Take the pan off the fire and scoop out the prawns.

Place these onto a serving dish and keep warm and apart.

Reduce the liquor left in the pan by half. Add the ginseng and then season the liquor to taste.

Serve the prawns and the liquor apart.

The liquor should be drunk after having eaten the prawns.

Preparation : 5 min • Cooking : 7 min
★ Very Easy ☆ Expensive

HEART OF PALM ACHARD

1 palm heart, fresh and trimmed
10 gm mustard seeds
5 gm turmeric powder
2 medium cleaned red chillies
100 ml vegetable oil
2 cloves crushed garlic
salt to taste

6 servings

Remove the bark from the fresh palm heart to reveal the tender centre.

Crush all the spices together with oil.

Cut the palm heart into slices and add to the spicy oil. Season to taste.

Allow to stand for 24 hours in the refrigerator before serving.

Preparation : 15 min
★ Very easy ☆ Cheap

CHICKEN AND LOBSTER CURRY

250 gm lobster meat
250 gm chicken meat
oil for frying
2 gm mint seeds
1 large onion, finely chopped
3 gm turmeric powder
5 gm curry powder
5 gm crushed root ginger
2 cloves crushed garlic
1 small fresh chilli, crushed
350 gm tomatoes, peeled and seeded
6 curry leaves
12 fresh coriander leaves,
finely chopped
1 spring onion, finely chopped
seasoning

4 servings

Cut the lobster and the chicken meat into bite-sized pieces. Cut the tomatoes into pieces.

Heat the oil in a pan.

Season the lobster and the chicken. 'Sweat' the lobster and the chicken separately; set aside and keep warm.

Place the mint seeds into the pan for 5 seconds. Add the onions, turmeric, curry, ginger, garlic and the chilli. Allow to cook for 1 minute, stirring constantly. Add the tomatoes and allow to simmer for a further minute.

Put the chicken and lobster into the mixture. Cook for 3 minutes, adding the curry leaves.

Pour in 2 cups of boiling water and cook for a further 5 minutes. Stir in the chopped coriander and spring onions. Season to taste and remove the curry leaves.

Serve with any white rice and chutney.

Preparation : 20 min • Cooking 15 min
★ Easy   ☆ Expensive

Chicken and Lobster Curry

PALM HEART AND PRAWN CURRY

1 fresh (or canned) palm heart
1 litre milk
oil for frying
250 gm cleaned prawns
1 large chopped onion
5 gm grated root ginger
5 cloves crushed garlic
60 gm curry powder
5 gm turmeric
1 sprig thyme
16 fresh coriander leaves
5 chopped spring onions
1 medium chopped green chilli
15 curry leaves
250 ml fish stock

4 servings

Cut the soft part of the palm heart into slices.

Bring the milk to the boil. Place the palm heart into the milk and cook for 5 minutes. Remove the palm heart from the milk and set aside keeping warm.

If using canned palm heart, remove from can and slice.

Heat the oil in a pan on a moderate heat and cook the prawns. Remove the prawns and set aside.

Add the onion, ginger, garlic, curry powder and turmeric to the remaining oil. Allow to cook on a slow heat for 2 or 3 minutes. Stir constantly so as not to burn.

Add the thyme, coriander, spring onions and chillies all finely chopped. Stir into the curry mix.

Add the prawns and the palm heart and curry leaves and mix thoroughly into the curry. Add the stock and stir well.

Cover the pan with a lid and cook gently for 3 minutes. Take out the curry leaves, coriander leaves and thyme. The curry sauce should not taste "grainy". If it does it needs more cooking. Season.

Preparation : 15 min • Cooking : 15 min
★ Easy   ☆ Expensive

FARATAS

1 kilo plain flour
125 ml warm water
60 ml vegetable oil
5 gm salt

8 servings

Place the flour and salt onto a table and make a well. Add the water little by little. Mix the water into the flour with your hands to form a smooth dough.

It is best to oil your hands to prevent the dough from sticking to your fingers.

Pour the oil over the dough and knead well for 10 minutes until the dough becomes soft and smooth.

Place in a bowl and cover with a clean cloth. Let the pastry rest for at least half an hour or more if possible.

Take small balls from the dough. Roll them out into circles about 20 cm in diameter. Brush a little oil on the top of each pastry circle. Turn the pastry over and brush the other side with oil. Fold the pastry into sections, taking the outside of the circle and fold to the centre of the circle.

Repeat this with the other side of the circle to meet the first fold. Turn the pastry over and fold again as above. This operation will leave you with a folded square. Do this until all the dough is used up. Cover with a cloth.

Heat the *tawa (or heavy iron pan) on a low heat. Brush the tawa with a very little oil.

Roll the folded square paste into a round again. Shape and place on the tawa. Cook for half a minute and turn it over to cook on the other side. Whilst the second side is cooking brush the top with oil.

Cook for a further half a minute and turn farata over again. Brush with oil and repeat the turning over and oiling until the farata is cooked.

Note: The farata is eaten mainly by the Indian community instead of rice. It is served with a variety of foods, eg. dholl, pumpkin, fricassee, bredes songe and various chutneys.

The farata is broken into pieces with the fingers and used to scoop up food. Knives and forks are not usually used.

If any faratas are left over, they are often eaten, with butter, the next day for breakfast.

*   A tawa is simply a round piece of metal. A frying pan may be used in the place of the tawa.

Preparation : 35 min • Cooking : 5 min
★ Easy   ☆ Cheap

SALTED FISH AND MANGO CHUTNEY

250 gm salted fish
oil for frying
1 medium onion, peeled
3 medium cleaned chillies
2 tblsp malt vinegar
1 pinch ground black pepper
1 tblsp olive oil

4 servings

Boil a pan of water. Place the salted fish in the water for 5 minutes.

Remove from the water, pat dry and cut into small pieces, removing the bones and the skin at the same time.

Heat the oil in the pan and fry the pieces of fish.

Chop the onion very finely. Cut the chillies into quarters, lengthways. Mix together the onion, chillies, olive oil, vinegar; add the fried salted fish.

Squeeze the water out of the grated mango and set the liquid aside. Add the mango to the fish mixture and stir in. Lastly, add the mango juice to the chutney.

Mix well and season to taste.

Preparation : 15 min • Cooking : 5 min
★ Easy   ☆ Cheap

CURRIED FISH
IN BANANA LEAVES

500 gm fish fillets
40 ml vegetable oil
100 gm grated fresh or dessicated coconut
120 gm chopped onions
3 cloves garlic, crushed
6 finely chopped fresh coriander leaves
2 large egg
4 finely chopped fresh curry leaves
2 tsp curry powder
1 tblsp coconut milk
60 gm crushed roasted peanuts
or cashew nuts
120 gm plain yoghurt
1 banana leaf cut into 20 cm squares
or aluminium foil

3 servings

Pre-heat the oven to 180°F (100°C).

Lightly poach the fish in a little water and mash thoroughly.

Heat the oil in a pan. Fry the coconut, onions and garlic until a golden brown then remove from the heat.

Mix the coconut mixture with the creamed fish. Add the rest of the ingredients to form a paste. Lightly grease the banana leaf square or foil.

Place some of the fish mixture on to the squares. Roll up each parcel, secure with a toothpick.

Place onto a tray and into the oven and cook for 15–20 minutes.

Serve with Creole Rice.

Preparation : 15 min • Cooking : 30 min
★ Easy   ☆ Cheap

DRY BEEF CURRY

600 gm fillet steak
40 ml vegetable oil
2 slices of bread cut into small cubes
12 small button onions
1 large cleaned onion finely chopped
2 cloves crushed garlic
10 gm crushed ginger
10 gm garam masala
2 medium tomatos each cut into six
1 tsp hot chilli sauce
25 gm grated fresh coconut
25 gm roasted peanuts
25 gm sultanas
1 hard boiled egg coarsely chopped
seasoning

4 servings

Cut the fillet steak into bite-sized pieces.

Heat 20 ml of the oil in a pan on a medium heat.

Place the beef into the pan and seal for about 2 minutes. Remove the beef from the pan and add the remaining oil.

Cook the button onions until very brown and quite crispy. Remove from the pan and keep apart.

Fry the bread cubes in the pan until a gold brown. Remove and keep apart.

Place the beef and its juices back into the pan and the onion, garlic and the ginger.

Cook for about 2 mins, add the garam masala and stir fry until mixed in. Stir in the tomato and the hot chilli sauce.

Cook for a further 3 mins on a gentle heat, add the remaining ingredients and heat through; serve with white rice.

The curry should be quite dry when ready to serve.

Preparation : 15 min • Cooking : 20 min
★ Easy   ☆ Moderate

BANANA AND CHEVRETTE CURRY

120 gm fresh chevrettes (or fresh shrimps)
3 cloves crushed garlic
5 gm crushed root ginger
5 gm ground coriander seeds
15 gm curry powder
2 tsp dried shrimp paste
5 gm turmeric
10 cm stalk lemon grass (citronelle)
oil for frying
1 large onion finely chopped
240 ml coconut milk
6 medium green bananas
4 spring onions finely chopped
12 leaves fresh coriander finely chopped
seasoning

4 servings

Wash the chevrettes well under running water.

Make a paste with the following ingredients: garlic, ginger, coriander, curry powder, shrimp paste, turmeric, and the lemon grass. Grind all the ingredients together in a mortar or a blender until it turns to a smooth paste.

Heat the oil in a pan on a moderate heat. Fry the onions until soft but not brown. Add the above spicy paste and fry for about 3 minutes, stirring constantly until it is fried.

Add the chevrettes and the coconut milk, stir in and cook for 3 more minutes.

Peel the bananas and cut them into bite-sized pieces.

Stir these into the mixture well and heat through for 2 more minutes. Season to taste.

Serve with Creole Rice and garnish with chopped spring onion and coriander leaves.

Preparation : 15 min • Cooking : 12 min
★ Very easy   ☆ Moderate

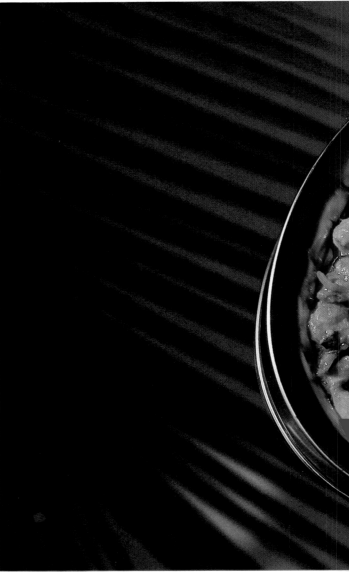

PEANUT CHUTNEY

250 gm roasted unsalted peanuts
3 small cleaned red chillies
15 clean fresh mint leaves
10 fresh coriander leaves
2 cloves crushed garlic
30 ml vegetable oil

Remove any skin from the peanuts. Place all of the ingredients into a blender and blend to form a smooth paste.

Preparation : 20 min
★ Very easy ☆ Cheap

COCONUT CHUTNEY

180 gm freshly grated coconut
or dessicated coconut
2 large fresh cleaned green chillies
30 ml olive oil
15 gm mustard seeds
10 gm crushed root ginger
15 gm curry powder
15 gm fresh mint leaves
finely chopped

4 servings

In a blender grind together the coconut and the chilli. Heat the oil in a pan. Add the mustard seeds to the pan and stir until the seeds begin to pop. Add to the seeds the ginger and curry and stir fry for 2 minutes. Allow to cool and then crush together very finely. Mix all the ingredients together with a fork and serve well chilled.

Preparation : 20 min • Cooking : 3 min
★ Very easy ☆ Cheap

Top: Lemon or Orange Achard (p. 117)
Opposite: Banana and Chevrette Curry
Bottom: Peanut Chutney, Coconut Chutney

CUCUMBER AND MINT CHUTNEY

1 medium onion
1 medium peeled cucumber
1 pinch salt
1 large cleaned fresh chilli
1 sprig fresh mint
1 tblsp malt vinegar
1 tblsp oil

3 servings

Clean and chop the onion very finely.
Remove the pips from cucumber and grate. Add the salt to the cucumber and chill for 2 hours.
Chop the chilli very finely.
Squeeze the water from the cucumber. Combine with the rest of the dry ingredients and mix together, then add the oil and vinegar.
Season to taste.

Preparation : 15 min
★ Very easy ☆ Cheap

KHORMA

400 gm beef topside
90 ml plain yoghurt
10 ml cooking oil
5 gm salt
4 cloves crushed garlic
5 gm crushed root ginger
5 gm crushed coriander seeds
2 large cleaned red chillies
1 large cleaned sweet green pepper
30 gm unsalted butter
1 large cleaned onion finely sliced
5 gm turmeric powder
100 gm garam masala
15 gm freshly grated coconut
2 large tomatoes, peeled and seedless
90 ml coconut milk

4 servings

Cut the beef into bite-sized pieces. Marinate in the yoghurt for 2 hours. Heat the oil in a pan on a low heat. Cook the beef and marinade slowly for 5 minutes. When the beef is ready, remove from the pan, keep apart and warm.
Put the butter in a pan and heat on a low fire. Fry the onions until soft, but not brown. Add the turmeric, garam masala and the coconut. Fry for two minutes; stirring all of the time. Slice the tomatoes and add these to the onion mix; stir in the garlic, ginger and coriander. Stir in the mixture for one minute. When complete add the already cooked meat.
Simmer for ten more minutes adding the coconut milk. When complete the khorma should be quite dry and of an attractive colour.

Preparation : 15 min • Cooking : 25 min
★ Very easy ☆ Moderate

CHEVRETTE CHUTNEY

150 gm chevrettes or fresh shrimps
2 small cleaned red chillies
2 cloves crushed garlic
5 gm crushed root ginger
4 small tomatoes, peeled and seeded

4 servings

Wash and clean the chevrettes; if using shrimps, remove the shells. Heat the oil in a pan on a moderate heat. Place the chevrettes into the oil and heat for 2 minutes, then add the remaining ingredients, cook for a few minutes, remove from the pan. Place all the ingredients into a blender. Blend on a low speed for 2 minutes.
Season to taste.

Note: Chevrettes are very small fresh water shrimps found in the running Mauritian streams.

Preparation : 5 min • Cooking 2 min
★ Very easy ☆ Moderate

116

TAMARIND CHUTNEY

60 gm boiling water
200 gm tamarind paste
10 gm red chilli powder
30 gm fine salt
60 gm castor sugar
40 ml malt vinegar

Pour the boiling water into the tamarind and allow to stand for 5 minutes.

Mix the chilli, salt, sugar and the vinegar together. Stir in the water and tamarind mixture.

Allow to cool and serve with hot samoosas.

Preparation : 10 min
★ Very easy ☆ Cheap

CURRY POWDER GARAM MASALA

30 gm coriander seeds
15 gm cummin
8 gm fennel
5 gm turmeric powder
3 gm cinnamon
3 gm cloves
3 gm cardamom
3 gm black peppercorns
5 gm mace
5 gm ground root ginger
5 gm dried curry leaves

Place all the ingredients into a frying pan. Put on a very low heat for 5 minutes and then remove.

Grind all the ingredients together in a blender on a low speed. Sieve through a fine sieve.

Store in an air-tight container.

Note: For many curries a basic curry powder mix is known as garam masala.

Whilst making a curry one can add individual spices to ones own taste as: crushed garlic, thyme, poppy seed, etc.

Try the above recipe and experiment by using your own choice of additional spices.

Preparation : 10 min
★ Very easy ☆ Moderate

LEMON OR ORANGE ACHARD

8 lemons or oranges
10 gm mustard seeds
2 medium cleaned red chillies
5 gm turmeric powder
2 cloves crushed garlic
120 ml vegetable oil
1 tsp malt vinegar
salt

6 servings

Remove the peel from the lemons or oranges. Ensure that there is no pith left on the peel, otherwise there will be a bitter taste.

Soak the peel in boiling water for at least 3 minutes. Cut the peel into strips. Leave the peel to dry in the sun for 1 day or in a warm oven for 2 hours.

Crush or liquidise the mustard seeds and the chillies. Mix the spices, oil and the vinegar together. Add the dried peel to the mixture and season to taste.

It is best to allow to marinate for 2 days before using.

Note: The drying of the peel is very important as it removes any water content that would spoil the achard over a period of days.

Achards can be kept for at least 10 days in the refrigerator.

Preparation : 40 min + drying time
★ Very easy ☆ Cheap

DEEP FRIED CRISPY BREAD FRUIT

1 peeled bread fruit
fine salt
liquid food colours
oil for frying

10 servings

Peel and slice the bread fruit as thin as possible. Cut the slices in half.

Sprinkle the slices with salt and allow to stand for 1 hour.

After standing, press the slices with a cloth to absorb any excess water.

Place the liquid colourings into a separate dish.

Colour the bread fruit and allow any excess liquid to drain.

Heat the oil until it is just beginning to smoke.

Deep fry the slices until crisp, but do not allow to brown. Drain.

Traditionally served with curry. If used for snacks the slices must be cut into bite-sized pieces.

Preparation : 10 min • Cooking : 3 min
★ Easy   ☆ Cheap

MIXED VEGETABLE ACHARD

15 gm mustard seeds
1 medium onion
5 gm root ginger
3 cloves crushed garlic
5 gm turmeric powder
1 small cauliflower
150 gm cabbage
150 gm carrots
150 gm fresh French beans
120 ml vegetable oil
4 medium fresh green chillies

6 servings

Crush the mustard seeds, onion and ginger with the garlic and turmeric.

Cut the cauliflower into flowerettes. Cut the cabbage, carrots and the French beans into a thick julienne. Blanch all of the vegetables in boiling water for about 30 seconds so they remain crunchy.

Drain any excess water. Mix the vegetables with the crushed spices and the oil.

Cut the chillies into four lengthways, clean and then add to the vegetables. Season to taste. Best used after having been kept in the refrigerator for 1 day, and may be kept up to 10 days. Serve with rougaille, bouillon or fricassees.

Preparation : 25 min • Cooking : 1 min
★ Very easy ☆ Cheap

TOMATO AND CORIANDER CHUTNEY

1 medium onion
6 medium tomatoes
1 large fresh green chilli cleaned,
finely chopped
15 gm finely chopped
coriander leaves
20 ml olive oil
30 ml malt vinegar
1 lemon squeezed for the juice

4 servings

Peel the onion and chop very finely. Slice the tomatoes and mix with the onion finely sliced, chilli and the coriander. Whisk the oil, vinegar and lemon juice together. Add to the tomato mixture and season to taste. Toss the salad gently but thoroughly.

Note: The coriander can be replaced with fresh mint, finely chopped.

Preparation : 10 min
★ Very easy ☆ Cheap

Left: Deep Fried Crispy Bread Fruit
Bottom left: Mixed Vegetable Achard
Bottom right: Kucha Mango

119

PORK CURRY WITH LYCHEES

300 gm tomatoes
1 kilo lean loin of pork
oil for frying
1 medium onion, finely chopped
30 gm curry powder
4 cloves crushed garlic
10 gm crushed root ginger
1 sprig fresh thyme
4 cloves
400 gm cleaned, pitted and halved
lychees
10 fresh curry leaves
20 fresh coriander leaves
finely chopped
20 fresh coriander leaves finely chopped
5 ml hot chilli sauce
seasoning

6 servings

Cut each tomato into 6 pieces. Cut the meat into bite-sized pieces.

Heat the oil in a pan. Fry the meat in the oil for 4 minutes.

Remove the meat from the pan and keep warm.

Add the onion to the same pan and fry until soft but not brown, then add the onions, the curry, garlic, ginger, thyme and cloves.

Cook for 2 minutes, stirring with a wooden spoon all the time.

Add the tomatoes and allow to cook slowly for 5 minutes, adding a little water if necessary.

Add the pork to the curry mixture and allow to cook for 20 minutes.

When the meat is tender add the lychees, curry leaves and the chopped coriander, cook for a further 5 minutes.

Remove the curry leaves and the sprig of thyme.

Add the chilli sauce and season to taste.

Serve with rice flavoured with elaichi (cardamom).

Preparation : 25 min • Cooking : 40 min
★ Easy   ☆ Moderate

GOAT CURRY

heart, lungs, liver and tripe
from a young goat
seasoning
1 litre fresh goat's blood
4 large sliced tomatoes
oil for frying
60 gm curry powder
5 gm fenugreek
1 large peeled onion, finely chopped
10 gm turmeric powder
10 curry leaves
15 gm crushed root ginger
4 cloves crushed garlic
2 medium fresh crushed chillies
10 fresh coriander leaves
1 sprig fresh thyme
4 spring onions

4 servings

Wash all of the meat under running cold water.

Cut the offal into bite-sized pieces.

Bring to the boil a pan of water, add some salt. Blanch the offal in the boiling water for about 2 minutes.

Pour the blood into a container and stir in some salt. The salt will thicken the blood.

Allow to stand in the refrigerator for 30 minutes.

Proceed to make the curry as for Chicken and Lobster Curry, but replacing the mint seeds in that recipe with the fenugreek.

When the offal is tender, cut the now thickened blood into small cubes.

Add these to the curry and stir in. This mixture should be quite thick.

Serve with Creole Rice and various chutneys, or dholl puree.

Note: This curry is normally served specially for the new year or the Indian New Year on the 14th January.

Preparation : 40 min • Cooking : 35 min
★ Difficult   ☆ Moderate

SALTED FISH WITH FRIED EGGS

800 gm salted fish
1 green mango
18 large green fresh chillies
2 large onions, peeled, finely chopped
oil for frying
12 medium eggs
6 servings watercress bouillon
coriander rice

6 servings

Boil a pan of water and remove from the fire.

Place the salted fish into the water for about 10 minutes.

Remove the skin from the green mango. Cut the chillies in half and remove the seeds.

Fry the onions in a little oil until brown. Remove from the pan.

Take the fish out of the water and pat dry. Flake the fish into very small pieces, removing any bones and skin.

Fry the fish until quite dry in a little oil, adding the chillies.

Mix together with the onions and grate the mango flesh into the mixture at the last minute. Keep warm.

Fry the eggs in a pan.

Serve the rice on a plate. Place the eggs on top of the rice, then spoon over the eggs, the fish, mango and onion mixture.

Serve with the watercress bouillon.

Preparation : 25 min • Cooking : 10 min
★ Very easy   ☆ Cheap

HOT CHILLI EGGS

6 large eggs
oil for deep frying
1 large cleaned onion finely chopped
2 cloves crushed garlic
5 gm crushed root ginger
5 gm dried shrimp paste
1 t sp Hot Chilli Sauce
2 large red chillies cleaned
5 gm citronelle (lemon grass)
5 gm tamarind
60 ml boiling water
5 gm sugar
5 gm turmeric powder
12 coriander leaves
12 curry leaves
1 spring fresh thyme
seasoning

3 servings

Boil the water in a pan and place in the eggs. Cook for 7 minutes.

Scoop out the egg and place into running cold water. When the eggs are cold, remove the shells. With a fork prick them gently.

Heat the oil and gently fry the eggs to a golden colour. Remove the eggs from the oil and set aside.

Heat a little oil in a pan and fry the onions until transparent. Add the crushed garlic and the ginger. Stir in. Add the rest of the ingredients and stir fry for about 2 minutes.

Place the eggs into the mixture and cook, gently turning all of the time. Cook until the eggs have absorbed all of the sauce. Serve hot.

Preparation : 10 min • Cooking : 10 min
★ Very easy   ☆ Cheap

THE MAGIC OF
THE EARTH

The rich tropical soil of Mauritius, being of volcanic origin, is highly productive. The combination of sun and rain weave their magic on anything planted and everything grows prolifically.

A visit to the exotic market in Port Louis is a *must*. One of its wings burnt down some time ago and as a result many stalls have crowded into the main central aisle, thus converting it into a kind of Arab souk. Any early morning, you can see the attractive displays of vegetables laid out for auction sale, amid much noisy and humorous bidding and chaffing. In fact, there are several such displays located in the markets in the major population centres, in the townships and even in such villages as Centre de Flacq, not far from *Saint Géran Sun*, especially if you call in on a Sunday, usually market day.

Rice, the staple diet of the country, does not grow in any great quantity on the island as production costs are too high, so this has made those vegetables that do grow well extremely popular.

Pumpkins are plentiful and make delicious soups, as well as a perfect puréed vegetable dish. *Patisson* (gem squash) are small in size and delicious when served with a knob of butter. *Lalo* (okra), usually known as lady's fingers and commonly grown here, are another tasty vegetable — especially when cut in cubes, deep-fried with a sprinkle of massala, Indian fashion, and served crisp.

The potatoes grown in Mauritius are not of very good quality, but hopefully this problem will be overcome in the future with the introduction of different varieties.

Due to the heat and humidity, lettuce is not very good and crisp, however radishes, spring onions and watercress make up handsomely for it, so one does have the basis for making some interesting salads.

One of the tourist attractions on the island is "The Coloured Earth", situated at Chamarel in the south-west, just 25 minutes drive from *La Pirogue Sun*. The mounds of earth of volcanic formation are a spectacular sight. When glistening and falling into perspective under a bright sun, they reflect seven different colours from pink to mauve. But do *not* visit on a cloudy day (which happens often, as it is mountainous country) or you will be disappointed. Our photographer, Gerald, had the bright idea of using the different layers of earth as a background for the colour plates in this chapter.

There is no voodoo, and very little magic, practised in Mauritius. However, the magic is there, as many visitors will testify.

CUCUMBER SALAD WITH GINGER

1 medium onion
1 cleaned cucumber
1 pinch salt
1 medium sweet green pepper
finely chopped
60 gm butter
1 tsp finely grated giner
1 plain yoghurt

2 servings

Clean and chop the onion very finely.

Remove the pips from the cucumber and grate, add the salt and chill for 2 hours.

Chop the pepper very finely.

Melt the butter gently in a pan taking care not to brown.

Add the onion, pepper and ginger to the butter.

Cook over low heat until the onion is tender but not brown, then remove from heat.

Squeeze the water from the cucumber, add to the onion mix and stir in.

Fold in the plain yoghurt.

Chill for 1 hour before serving.

Preparation : 10 min • Cooking : 5 min
★ Very easy   ☆ Cheap

BRAISED RED CABBAGE

60 gm unsalted butter, softened
1 medium red cabbage
2 large cooking apples, peeled
1 large cleaned onion
60 ml cider vinegar
10 ml honey
120 ml red wine
120 ml chicken stock
1 pinch salt

6 servings

Butter a casserole dish with the butter. Pre-heat the oven to 350°. Clean the cabbage and cut into six wedges. Cut off the stalk at the base of the wedge. Cut the apples each into six and remove the core. Cut the onion into slices. Place the cabbage; apples and onions into the casserole. Bring the rest of the ingredients to the boil. Pour into the casserole. Cover the casserole with silver foil and place in the oven. Cook for 30 minutes, or until the cabbage is tender but still firm.

Serve with the apples; onions and spoon over the stock.

Preparation : 15 min • Cooking : 35 min
★ Very easy   ☆ Cheap

HOT AND SPICY PICKLED GHERKIN CUCUMBER

1 kilo fresh gherkin cucumbers
30 gm sea salt
15 ml sesame oil
1 medium red chilli, cleaned and
shredded
15 gm root ginger, shredded
1 tot white rum
60 ml malt vinegar
10 gm fresh pink peppercorns
50 gm sugar

6 servings

Cut the tips off both ends of the gherkins. Cut each one into 6, lengthways. Mix with the sea salt and let them rest for 20 minutes. Rinse under running cold water and drain. Heat the oil in a pan. Add the shredded chilli and root ginger. Stir fry for about 30 seconds. Add the rum, vinegar, sugar and the fresh peppercorns. Remove from the heat and pour over the gherkins.

Refrigerate before serving.

Preparation : 30 min • Cooking : 1 min
★ Very easy   ☆ Cheap

Previous page: Bulgare Salad (p. 137)

STUFFED COURGETTE FLOWERS

6 courgettes with the flower still attached
1 medium onion cleaned and finely
chopped
30 gm unsalted butter
20 gm fresh pine nuts
100 gm finely minced chicken meat
100 gm finely minced lamb
10 gm chopped parsley
3 gm allspice powder
1 pinch freshly ground black pepper
1 clove finely chopped mint
seasoning

180 ml curry sauce

3 servings

Clean the courgette carefully so as not to break off the flower.

Heat the butter gently in a pan. Cook the onions in the butter, but do not brown. Cook the pine nuts with the onion for just 3 minutes.

To the onions, add the minced chicken and lamb. Stir fry for about five minutes. Add to the meat the spices and the herbs.

Combine the ingredients thoroughly and season to taste.

Place the mixture into a piping bag.

Gently open the flowers and pipe enough mixture to fill the flowers by two thirds.

Fold the flower petals of each courgette over one another, thus covering the mixture.

Place the courgettes into a Chinese steamer. Allow to steam for 15 minutes. It is nice to add some fine herbs to the water of the steamer.

When cooked remove carefully from the steamer.

Cut the end of the courgette into fine slices lengthways thus creating a fan.

Pour the curry sauce into a blender, recommended on page 48.

Place the sauce onto a plate and then the courgettes to top. Serve hot.

Preparation : 20 min • Cooking : 30 min
★ Difficult ☆ Moderate

WAYS TO MAKE COCONUT MILK

Coconut milk is an essential base for a wide range of dishes in tropical climates — from chilli-hot curries to rich desserts.

Recipes will call for the thick, or first, milk or thin milk and it is important to differentiate between the two.

Coconut milk can be bought as compressed cakes.

These are dissolved in warm water to make the required thickness.

If the compressed cakes are not available, there are three different ways of obtaining the same results:

Take 150 gm of fresh coconut, remove the brown skin and grate.

Place in a liquidizer with 250 ml of water or milk. Blend on high speed until a smooth liquid is obtained.

Strain through a piece of muslin. The result is thick coconut milk.

For thin coconut milk add a further 125 ml of hot milk or water before putting through muslin.

Fresh coconut milk can be frozen into cubes for future use.

Use as many cubes as necessary.

PEANUT AND CELERY SALAD WITH PINEAPPLE

4 sticks cleaned celery
½ small cleaned pineapple
120 gm cheddar cheese
2 eating apples
60 gm cooked ham
60 gm roasted unsalted peanuts
60 ml plain yoghurt

3 servings

This is a good salad for calorie watchers — light, crisp and healthy but the yoghurt and peanuts make it a satisfying meal.

Cut the celery and pineapple into small, even dice. Cut the cheese, apple, ham and celery into small pieces.

Add the peanuts and mix together. Pour in the yoghurt and stir. Or, instead of the yoghurt, if you prefer you can use a very light mayonnaise. Season to taste.

Preparation : 5 min
★ Very easy   ☆ Cheap

Bottom: Peanut and Celery Salad with Pineapple – Opposite: Black Lentils

BLACK LENTILS

250 gm black lentils
15 fresh curry leaves
1 sprig fresh thyme
oil for frying
2 large tomatoes, skinned and seeded
2 large onions, peeled and chopped
3 cloves garlic, crushed
5 gm root ginger, crushed
5 gm chopped parsley

4 servings

Cook the lentils in a pressure steamer, in boiling water for 2 hours or with the curry leaves, the thyme and water. Watch carefully, adding more water if necessary. Stir occasionally. Cook until quite soft. Remove from the cooker and remove the leaves and the thyme.

Heat the oil in a pan on a low heat.

Cut the tomatoes into pieces. Cook the onion with the garlic and the ginger. Add the tomatoes and heat through, then add the chopped parsley. Pour in the lentils, and stir into the onions and tomatoes.

Season to taste.

Note: Red lentils may also be cooked in the same way.

Preparation : 10 min • Cooking : 30 min
★ Very easy ☆ Cheap

DHOLL PURI

1 kilo dholl (yellow split peas)
500 ml water
5 gm turmeric
1 kilo plain flour
5 gm salt

12 servings

Method 1:

Wash and clean the dholl thoroughly under running water. Cook the dholl in the water with the turmeric and the salt. Allow to simmer until the dholl is soft but not creamy, about 35 minutes. When the dholl is ready, strain from the water. Retain both, keeping them separate.

Place the flour onto a table and form a well in the centre. Slowly pour some of the dholl water into the flour. Form a smooth paste and knead for a good 8 minutes, until the dough becomes supple. Put the paste into a bowl and cover. Allow to stand for half an hour.

Take the dholl and crush or blend into a smooth paste.

After allowing the paste to rest for 1 hour, take sufficient of it to form a medium sized ball. Oil your hands and place the ball into your palm. Cut the ball open and place some of the crushed dholl inside. Roll the ball in the palm of your hands to close the cut, encasing the dholl.

Place the ball of paste onto a floured board and roll into a circle, 20 cm in diameter.

From this point cook on the tawa (or heavy iron pan) as for Faratas.

Method 2:

Cook the dholl until it is a creamy consistency. Strain in a fine strainer, removing as much water as possible. Mix the creamy dholl mixture with the flour to form a smooth paste. Knead well. If the paste is too sticky, add more flour. Allow the paste to rest for 1 hour.

Oil your hands and roll a ball of the paste into your palm. Place the ball of paste onto a floured board. Roll into a circle, 20 cm in diameter.

Cook as for Faratas.

Method 2 produces a heavier dholl puri.

Note: The puri can be eaten with any curried vegetable dish, with achards or chutneys.

Preparation : 30 min • Cooking : 45 min
★ Difficult   ☆ Cheap

MANGO KUCHA

10 gm mustard seeds
2 cloves garlic
4 green mangoes
2 fresh green chillies
15 ml vegetable oil
5 gm turmeric
5 gm salt   6 servings

Crush the mustard seeds and the garlic separately.

Peel and grate the mangoes, press all the excess liquid from them.

Cut the chillies each into 4 and clean.

Heat the oil in a pan to a moderate heat.

Place the garlic, chillies and the turmeric in the pan. Stir continuously for ½ minute.

Add the crushed mustard seeds and the mango.

Mix well and remove from the pan, season to taste.

To conserve for 3 or 4 days just ad 1 tsp of malt vinegar.

Note: The difference between achard and kucha is that the kucha is grated and squeezed with only a little oil and the achard is cut into strips and more oil is used in the preparation.

Preparation : 10 min
★ Very easy   ☆ Cheap

FRICASSEE OF DHOLL

500 gm dholl (yellow split peas)
5 curry leaves
3 large tomatoes, peeled and seeded
50 gm ghee
1 small onion, finely chopped
10 gm turmeric
10 gm crushed root ginger
3 cloves garlic, crushed
10 gm cummin, crushed
2 litres water

8 servings

Soak dholl for 2 hours in cold water to cover. Cook the dholl in the water on a moderate heat with the curry leaves until it becomes a puree, but not too thick. Set aside and keep warm. Chop the tomatoes into pieces.

Heat the ghee in a pan. Fry the onions until soft but not brown. Add the turmeric, ginger and the crushed garlic. Stir in and cook for 1 minute, then add the cummin and the tomatoes. Cook for a further minute, stirring constantly.

Add the dholl puree to the above mixture.

Season to taste and allow to boil gently for 5 minutes.

To serve, sprinkle with chopped coriander and serve with Coconut Chutney or Tomato and Coriander Chutney and Delicious Rice.

Preparation : 20 min • Cooking : 2½ h
★ Very easy   ☆ Cheap

ROAST BREAD FRUIT

1 bread fruit
vegetable oil for frying
salt

4 servings

Pre-heat the oven to 250°F (140°C).
Peel the bread fruit.
Cut into reasonable sizes as per roast potatoes.
Cut into a barrel shape with a sharp knife.
Heat a little oil in a tray.
Season the bread fruit.
Place the bread fruit into the oil and turn over, covering with the oil.
Then cook in the oven until crisp outside and soft inside, approx. 25 minutes.
Serve as one would serve roast potatoes.

Note: They can also be cut as chips and deep-fried, or straw potatoes, crisps, or boiled and served with butter.

Preparation : 10 min • Cooking : 25 min
★ Very easy   ☆ Cheap

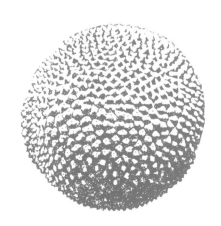

CREOLE RICE

A popular commercial version
1 kilo basmati rice
1¼ litres water
10 gm turmeric
4 small red pimentos
4 small sweet green peppers
1 large onion
6 large tomatoes
oil for frying
10 gm chopped parsley
100 gm sliced mushrooms
3 tsp garden peas

10 servings

Cook the rice exactly as for Creole Rice.

When cooked, fold in the turmeric. Dice the red pimentos and green peppers finely. Chop the onion roughly, and cut the tomatoes into 6.

Heat the oil in a pan. Fry the chopped onion for 1 minute. Do not allow to colour. Add the rest of the ingredients to the onion. Fry gently for about 1 minute.

Fold all these ingredients into the rice.

Basmati rice is best for this dish because it has more flavour.

Preparation : 10 min • Cooking : 45 min
★ Very easy ☆ Cheap

BEETROOT LEAVES "TOUFFE"

1 kilo young beetroot leaves
oil for frying
1 large peeled onion, coarsely chopped
2 small cleaned green chillies,
coarsely chopped
5 gm crushed root ginger
2 cloves crushed garlic
seasoning

4 servings

Remove the beetroot leaves from the stalks, as the stalks make the dish bitter. Wash under running water and dry.

Heat the oil in a pan. Fry the onions until soft but not brown. Stir in the chillies, ginger and the garlic. Toss in the beetroot leaves. Cook for 2 minutes, stirring constantly. Season to taste. Serve with white Creole Rice mixed with finely chopped parsley or Faratas, salted fish and mango chutney.

Preparation : 5 min • Cooking : 5 min
Very Easy ☆ Cheap

Bottom left: Fricassee of Haricots Blancs (p. 132)
Top left: Cantonese Rice (p. 132)
Top right: Creole Rice
Bottom right: Beetroot Leaves "Touffe"

CANTONESE RICE

6 large Chinese mushrooms
1 large onion
2 large eggs
60 gm peeled prawns
60 gm cooked beef
60 gm roast pork
4 spring onions
500 gm cooked white rice
1 tsp sesame oil
15 ml soya sauce
90 gm sliced Chinese sausage
30 gm chopped Chinese garlic (or queue d'ail)
6 fresh coriander leaves
oil for frying

6 servings

Soak the Chinese mushrooms for 20 minutes in water. Finely chop the onion.

Beat the eggs with a little salt. Chop the prawns, beef and the pork into small dice. Finely chop the spring onions.

Fry the rice in the oil on a low heat until the grains are well coated, set aside.

Place the eggs in an oiled pan. Swirl around the pan to form a pancake. Cook until firm. Remove from the pan and cut into strips.

Cook the prawns until pink and remove from the pan.

Cook the onions in the pan until soft.

Place the beef and the pork into an oiled pan. Cook for 2 minutes, add the sesame oil. Slice the mushrooms caps finely, (discard stalks) and add to the onion and the meat. Stir fry for one minute, adding the above ingredients, except the egg. Splash in the soya sauce.

Add the sausage, rice, and prawns to the rest of the ingredients. Stir fry again on a very high heat until hot.

Transfer to a serving dish. Place the strips of egg and coriander on top of the rice.

Preparation : 15 min • Cooking : 8 min
★ Very easy   ☆ Moderate

FRICASSEE OF HARICOTS BLANCS

1 kilo white haricot beans (or red)
250 gm lamb neck chopped into pieces
oil for frying
10 gm cummin seeds, crushed
2 large onions coarsely chopped
2 cloves crushed garlic
1 sprig fresh thyme
10 gm root ginger, crushed
1 cinnamon stick
6 crushed cloves
4 medium cleaned chillies each cut into 4
15 gm parsley
2 bay leaves
6 whole peeled tomatoes

6 servings

Soak the beans in water overnight. Next morning strain the beans from the water.

Place the lamb into a pot of clean water. Bring to the boil, then add the beans with a little salt. Cook in a pressure cooker for 20 minutes.

If cooked in a saucepan with water, cooking time is about 2½ hours.

Place the oil into a pan on a low heat. Add the cummin, onion, garlic, thyme and ginger. Cook for 1 minute.

Add the rest of the ingredients and cook for three minutes. Add the beans to the onion, mix and cook for 5 minutes. Remove the bay leaf, thyme, parsley and cinnamon stick.

Serve with Creole Rice and Chevrette Chutney.

Preparation : 25 min • Cooking : 30 min
★ Easy   ☆ Cheap

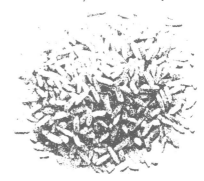

DELICIOUS RICE

4 cups basmati or long grain rice
150 gm unsalted butter
2 tsp salt

4 servings

Pre-heat the oven to moderate.

Wash the rice thoroughly in cold water; removing any impurities. Boil the rice in a large pan on high heat for 10 minutes in boiling water with the salt and 30 gm of the butter. Remove the rice and drain off the water.

Melt 60 gm of butter in the bottom of a non-stick pan and add the rice, spreading evenly.

Make 4 holes of smallish diameter equally spaced about 5 cm from the edge of the pan and insert a wedge of the remaining butter into each hole. Place a clean kitchen cloth over the pot to absorb the steam and place a lid on top.

Place in the oven and leave to cook for 45 to 50 minutes.

Note: The test of delicious rice is a good "tadig" which is the name given to the crisp golden brown crust of rice at the bottom of the pan. The rice may be turned out to reveal this golden brown crust.

Delicious Rice may be served with a variety of dishes in this book or simply with plain yoghurt.

Note: One can mix tomato puree with the butter. That is placed into the 4 holes in the rice before putting in the oven.

Preparation : 5 min • Cooking : 45/50 min
★ Easy   ☆ Cheap

PILAW A LA MAURICIENNE

350 gm long grain rice
oil for frying
250 gm chicken meat cut into small pieces
250 gm lean pork meat cut into small pieces
4 beef sausages cut into small pieces
2 large cleaned onions
3 gm turmeric powder
4 large tomatoes peeled and seeded each cut into 6 pieces
2 pinch ground cinnamon
4 cloves
seasoning

4 servings

Chop the onions very finely.

Heat the oil in a pan on a low heat. Cook the chicken, pork and the sausages separately. Keep apart after the cooking and keep warm.

Heat a little more oil in the pan. Cook the onions until soft. Add the turmeric and stir in. Pour in the rice and mix in with the onions. Add the tomatoes and stir in.

Pour in the water and bring to the boil. Allow to simmer for 10 minutes. Stir in the chicken, pork, cinnamon and the cloves. Continue cooking for about 30 minutes.

When cooked, add the sausages and season to taste.

Preparation : 10 min • Cooking : 40 min
★ Very easy   ☆ Cheap

133

COURGETTE BLOSSOMS

18 courgette blossoms in full bloom
2 large eggs
120 gm plain flour, 10 gm salt
15 gm baking powder
½ clove crushed garlic
10 gm chopped basil leaves

6 servings

Wash the courgette blossoms very carefully. Place onto a towel to dry.

Beat the eggs together with the salt, sifted flour and the baking powder. If necessary add water to make the correct consistency. Add the garlic and basil, and season.

Heat the oil to very hot. Dip the courgette blossoms one at a time in the batter and deep fry until a golden brown. Remove from the oil and drain onto paper towels. Serve hot.

Note: Flowers from the pumpkin or patisson (gem squash) may also be used.

Preparation : 10 min • Cooking : 10 min
★ Very easy   ☆ Cheap

Bottom left: Courgette Blossoms
Bottom right: Ratatouille
Opposite: Vegetable Chop Suey (p. 136)

RATATOUILLE

2 gm medium aubergine
1 small green sweet pepper
1 small red sweet pepper
75 ml olive oil
1 medium onion, finely chopped
1 medium leek, cleaned and chopped
3 cloves crushed garlic
1 small patisson, (gem squash) sliced
4 large tomatoes, skinned and seeded
2 medium courgettes, sliced
salt

6 servings

Slice the aubergines, sprinkle with salt and set aside for 10 minutes.

Clean and chop the red and green pepper. Rinse the aubergine and dry.

Heat the oil in a pan. Fry the onions, leeks and the garlic until tender but not brown.

Add the aubergine to the onions. Cook for 2 minutes. Add the rest of the ingredients and cook until tender but not soft.

Season to taste.

Note: Sliced black olives may be added before seasoning.

Preparation : 15 min • Cooking : 8 min
★ Very easy   ☆ Cheap

VEGETABLE CHOP SUEY

4 black Chinese mushrooms
1 small sweet green pepper
1 small sweet red pepper
¼ fresh pineapple
1 large peeled carrot
1 medium cleaned onion
60 gm bamboo shoots
10 gm cornflour mixed with a little water
oil for frying
4 baby corn cobs cut into 4
4 oyster mushrooms
60 gm fresh bean shoots
10 ml oyster sauce
30 ml soya sauce

2 servings

Soak the Chinese mushrooms in water for 30 minutes. Cut the peppers in half and remove the seeds. Cut the pineapple into triangles; slice the carrot quite thinly, slice the peppers into a fine julienne, cut the onions into fine slices, cut the bamboo shoots into a fine julienne, cut the mushrooms into 4 pieces each.

Dissolve the cornflour in 10 ml of water.

Heat the oil in a wok or a pan until very hot. Put the peppers, onions and the carrots into the oil and stir fry for 30 seconds. Add the rest of the vegetables and stir fry for a further minute.

Add the oyster sauce and soya sauce. Pour in the cornflour and allow to cook for 30 seconds.

Season to taste.

Note: The heat during this whole operation must be high.

Preparation : 35 min • Cooking : 4 min
★ Very easy ☆ Cheap

STUFFED COURGETTES

3 medium courgettes
30 ml oil for frying
200 gm minced lean pork
2 chicken livers finely chopped
½ tsp sesame oil
2 chevrettes
80 gm finely chopped mushrooms
seasoning
water

6 servings

Slice both ends of the courgettes, put aside the six ends and retain. Keeping them whole, scoop out the seeds of the courgettes using a small knife.

Heat some oil in a pan. Mix the meat, livers, sesame oil, chevrettes and the mushrooms together, stir fry in hot oil for 2 minutes. Season to taste.

Stuff the courgette with this filling. Replace the ends of the courgette, secure with toothpicks.

Heat the oil in a pan. Add the courgette and fry for about 3 minutes, turning constantly. Remove the courgette from the oil and drain.

Place enough water into a pan to cover the courgettes. Bring to the boil, add some salt.

Put the courgette into water and allow to simmer for about 8 minutes. The courgette by then should be very tender.

Remove the toothpicks and cut into slices.

Preparation : 20 min • Cooking : 12 min
★ Easy ☆ Cheap

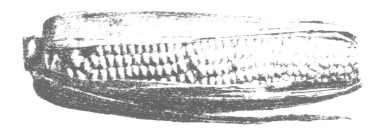

BULGARE SALAD

3 large tomatoes
1 medium sweet red pepper (capsicum)
1 medium sweet green pepper (capsium)
1 medium onion
10 ml malt vinegar
20 ml olive oil
1 lemon squeezed for the juice
6 crushed caraway seeds

4 servings

Remove the skin from the tomatoes by plunging them briefly into boiling water, then peel.

To take the skin from the peppers, hold them over a gas flame on a fork, turning them until charred.

The skin then peels away easily. The grilling gives the peppers a distinctive taste.

Cut in half and remove the seeds from the peppers and the tomatoes. Cut into coarse slices.

Peel and slice the onion finely. Mix all together.

Shake together the malt vinegar, lemon juice and olive oil with the crushed caraway seeds and pour dressing over chilled salad ingredients.

Season to taste.

Preparation : 10 min
★ Very easy   ☆ Cheap

PLAIN RICE

1 kilo basmati rice
1¼ litres water
seasoning

8 portions

Wash the rice several times in water.

Place the rice in a pan with the water and season. Place a lid on the pan. Bring to the boil on a fast heat.

When cooked put on a very low heat. The rice will dry slowly.

Preparation : 10 min • Cooking 45 min
★ Very easy   ☆ Cheap

VEGETABLE OMELETTE

60 gm bamboo shoots
60 gm roast pork
8 spring onion shoots
6 large eggs
1 tsp sesame oil
15 gm cornflour
2 tblsp water
oil for frying
20 gm soaked Chinese mushrooms
1 small grated carrot
5 gm grated root ginger
15 gm bean shoots
1 medium fresh red chilli
½ tsp soya sauce
1 sprig fresh coriander leaves
seasoning

3 servings

Cut the bamboo shoots and the roast pork into fine shreds. Chop the spring onions into small pieces.

Beat the eggs lightly with a little salt, and season. Add the sesame oil to the eggs. Mix the cornflour with the water and add to the egg mix.

Place the oil in a pan on a fast heat. Place the vegetables and the pork in the pan with the soya sauce. Fry lightly until the vegetables are only slightly softened. Pour in the eggs and stir the vegetables evenly through the egg. Cook on low heat until omelette is firm underneath.

Turn omelette over and cook on the other side.

When cooked garnish with a sprig of fresh coriander leaves and a chopped red chilli.

Preparation : 10 min • Cooking : 10 min
★ Very easy   ☆ Cheap

137

SWEET

FANTASIES

With sugar in sweet, prolific abundance throughout Mauritius, the dessert course has always been considered an integral part of the whole structure of a meal.

Over 90 percent of arable land in Mauritius (aptly called the sugar bowl) is used for the cultivation of sugarcane. On the rolling plains, and up the mountain slopes, one can see the mauve feathery-flowered tops swaying in the gentle breeze — a lovely and tranquil sight.

Most Mauritian children grow up biting into the sugarcane stems to extract the sweet juices. The total crop ranges from between 600 to 700 thousand tons, depending on how much damage the periodic cyclones have done during the summer months. The plant grows to a height of three metres and is only replanted every six years or so.

Over 500,000 tons are exported annually to the European Economic Community at a price fixed by agreements drawn under the Lomé Convention — usually much higher than the world market price. The rest goes to North America or, of course, is used for local consumption — around 50,000 tons of it — which makes Mauritians indeed the highest per capita consumers of sugar in the world.

The delicious tropical fruits which are freely available are a perfect basis for light fruit sorbets, which make a welcome change from vanilla and chocolate. Lychee, mango, passion fruit, watermelon and even avocado are the exotic fruits used in producing the perfect light ending to a meal, or a palate-cleanser between courses.

Without doubt the French influence prevails when it comes to desserts. *Crème caramel*, or the Mauritian version *Crème coco*, with the addition of toasted coconut to the caramel, is a firm favourite, as is the Mauritian alternative to the French *vacherin*, which is a light meringue case filled with lashings of cream, ice cream and a selected fruit or two. The ladies, shivering in the diplomatic belt of Floreal on the central plateau of Mauritius, compete with each other to produce the largest and tastiest *vacherin*.

One dish which is easier to prepare than it seems at first glance is *banana flambé*. This is a truly Mauritian dish, blending bananas with sugar, butter and lime juice, the whole flamed in Mauritian rum.

The desserts in this book are photographed with some interesting varieties of shells. Visitors to Mauritius are often interested in taking shells home as souvenirs of their stay, but they should make sure of obtaining official clearance before leaving.

DHOLL FRITTERS

100 gm yellow lentils
½ tsp turmeric powder
30 gm freshly grated coconut
60 gm sugar
1 cup coconut milk
1 egg
60 gm plain flour
1 pinch salt
water
oil for deep frying

10 servings

Wash the lentils well. Place in a pan and cover with water to about one and half inches above the level of the lentils. Bring to the boil and cook until very soft. Watch and stir constantly to prevent burning. Drain very well. The dholl should be of a very thick consistency.

Add the turmeric powder to the sugar and mix together. Add to the dholl. Stir into the dholl the grated coconut, and the coconut milk, and allow to cool.

Form small balls in the palm of your hand with the dholl mixture.

If the dholl is not firm enough add a little cornflour. Make a paste with the flour, egg, salt and water. Beat to make a smooth batter and pass through a sieve. Leave to stand for twenty minutes.

Heat the oil to smoking point and then lower the heat.

Drop the dholl balls into the batter. Lift out with a fork and allow the batter to drain a little.

Drop the battered dholl into the oil and fry to a golden brown. Scoop out and drain well. Serve hot.

The dholl fritters can also be rolled in caster sugar after being cooked.

Preparation : 15 min • Cooking : 45 min
★ Easy   ☆ Cheap

PAW PAW AND AVOCADO PANCAKE

For the pancake:
75 gm maize flour
75 gm plain flour (or 150 gm plain flour)
1 pinch salt
1 pinch nutmeg
¼ litres milk
50 gm unsalted butter
2 eggs

6 servings

For the filling:
2 large avocados
200 gm fresh paw paw
10 gm olive oil
1 lemon squeezed for the juice
30 gm sugar

Sieve together the flour, salt and the nutmeg. Beat in the eggs. Whisk in the milk and pour through a fine sieve. Melt the butter and whisk in well. Allow to stand for 1 hour.

Peel and remove the stone of the avocado. Clean the paw paw and cut into small dice. Crush the avocado to a puree. Mix the two fruits together.

Pour over the olive oil and lemon juice, mix in gently, then add the sugar.

Continue to make pancakes in the normal manner. Put the filling on one edge of the pancake, fold over and sprinkle with sugar.

Serve hot.

Preparation : 10 min • Cooking : 10 min
★ Very easy   ☆ Cheap

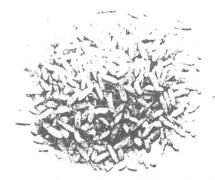

Previous page: Orange Caramel Cream (p. 145)

JACKFRUIT FRITTERS

750 gm cleaned jackfruit pieces
100 gm brown sugar
3 cups warm water
250 gm rice flour
2 tsp baking powder
pinch of salt
125 gm grated fresh coconut
oil for deep frying

6 servings

Dissolve the sugar in the warm water and allow to cool, set aside.

Mix together the rice flour, baking powder, salt and the coconut. Pour in the sugar syrup and beat to make a smooth batter.

Allow to stand for 10 minutes.

Heat the oil to smoking point then lower the heat. Dip the jackfruit pieces into the batter and fry to a deep golden brown. Remove from the oil and allow to drain. Sprinkle with sugar.

Note: Apples, banana or pineapple may be used in the place of jackfruit.

The stones from the jackfruit can be cooked in boiling water for about 15 minutes. Drain and allow to dry. They are then ready for eating.

Preparation : 15 min • Cooking : 10 min
★ Very easy   ☆ Cheap

CANDIED PAW PAW

800 gm green paw paw
150 gm honey
150 sugar
2 tsp malt vinegar
250 ml water

6 servings

Peel the skin off of the green paw paw. Cut in half and remove the seeds. Cut the paw paw into 1.25 cm thick batons. Mix the rest of the ingredients together.

Place in a pan and bring to the boil. Add the paw paw and cook gently for 20 minutes.

The sauce by now should be reduced by ⅔ and the paw paw quite tender. Remove the paw paw from the thick syrup and place on a serving plate.

Pour the remaining sauce over the candied paw paw.

Preparation : 10 min • Cooking : 20 min
★ Very easy   ☆ Cheap

BANANA BREAD

1 kilo plain flour
30 gm baking powder
1 kilo ripe bananas
1 kilo brown sugar
8 large whole eggs
240 ml olive oil
250 ml milk
½ tsp salt

3 × 1 lb loaves

Sieve the flour; salt and the baking powder together.

Puree the ripe bananas. Mix the banana with the sugar and beat well. Add the eggs slowly, beating all the time.

Fold in the sieved flour mixture, then add the oil and milk and fold in well.

Pour the mixture into greased and lined tins. Bake at 275°F (150°C) for approx. 2 hours.

Cool before turning out.

Note: ½ teaspoon banana essence may be added if a stronger flavour is preferred.

Preparation : 15 min • Cooking : 2 h
★ Very easy   ☆ Cheap

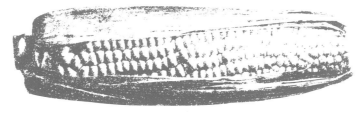

BANANA TART

1 tin condensed milk
350 gm sweet shortcrust pastry
200 ml whipped cream
60 gm soft brown sugar
20 gm instant coffee
3 large bananas

8 servings

Place the tin of condensed milk into a pan of water and simmer for about 3 hours. Never allow to boil dry, otherwise the tin will explode!

Pre-heat oven to moderate.

Roll out the pastry and place into a 20 cm tart mould. Cook in the oven, placing beans or rice into some foil and then onto the pastry. When cooked, remove from oven. Take out foil holding the beans.

After 3 hours remove the tin of condensed milk from the pan. Allow to cool for 1 hour. This is very important.

Open the tin, and spread the contents onto the base of the baked tart. Slice the bananas and spread them on top of the mixture in the tart. Cover with the whipped cream.

Sprinkle the soft brown sugar and instant coffee on top. Serve chilled.

Preparation : 10 min • Cooking : 4½ h
(including the condensed milk)
★ Difficult   ☆ Cheap

RUM AND CHOCOLATE MOUSSE

150 gm dark chocolate
90 ml fresh double cream
4 egg whites
15 gm sieved cocoa powder
15 gm sieved instant coffee
180 gm sugar, 2 tots dark rum

4 servings

Place the chocolate in a bowl with the cream, then place the bowl over warm water and stir whilst the chocolate is melting. Whisk the egg whites to a snow. Add the cocoa and the instant coffee. Pour in the sugar very slowly, whisking continually. Add the rum to the chocolate mixture and beat in. Put half the egg whites into the chocolate and fold in gently with a wooden spoon, then repeat with the other half of the egg whites. Mix gently until the egg white is fully incorporated and no white can be seen in the mixture. Place into champagne glasses. Refrigerate for at least 30 minutes before serving.

Preparation : 20 min
★ Easy   ☆ Cheap

Bottom left: Banana Tart
Bottom right: Rum & Chocolate Mousse
Opposite: Surprise for Juliette

SURPRISE FOR JULIETTE

For the bun:
125 ml milk
60 gm unsalted butter
1 pinch salt
1 pinch sugar
90 gm plain flour
3 small eggs

8 servings

Place the milk, butter, salt and the sugar into a pan. Bring to the boil and simmer until the butter is melted. Sieve the flour, then pour it into the hot milk.

Beat very hard with a wooden spoon.

Cook the paste on a low heat for a full minute, beating constantly. Remove the pan from the heat.

Beat the eggs into the paste, one at a time.

Pre-heat the oven to 250°F (140°C), placing an empty oven-proof dish on the floor of the oven.

Grease and flour a tray. Pipe the paste onto the tray, in a bun, then place the tray into the oven. Pour a glass of water into the empty dish in the oven. Cook the buns for approx. 20 minutes or until firm.

Remove from the oven and allow to cool.

(See following page)

Surprise for Juliette (continued)

For the filling:
8 balls passion fruit ice cream (or another flavour if preferred)
120 gm sieved icing sugar
sliced melon
sliced watermelon
sliced mango
strawberries
8 leaves fresh mint, chopped
250 gm passion fruit juice
30 gm sugar

Cut the bun in half. Place one ball of the ice cream in the bun.

Replace the lid and dust with the icing sugar. Mark the icing sugar with a very hot skewer in a criss-cross pattern. Place the sliced fruit decoratively along the centre cut of the bun.

Mix the mint, passion fruit and the sugar together. Pour onto the plates and place the bun in the centre.

Preparation : 45 min • Cooking : 20 min
★ Difficult   ☆ Moderate

RICE WITH MILK

100 gm basmati rice or any long grain rice
1 litre water
1 litre milk
1 tin condensed milk
3 elaichi (cardamom) seeds
45 gm roasted flaked almonds
rose water to taste

4 servings

Half cook the rice then drain well.

Boil the milk in a pan and add the cooked rice. Pour in the concentrated milk and the elaichi, cook for 15 minutes on a low heat. Add rose water to taste.

Serve warm, sprinkled with almonds.

Preparation : 15 min • Cooking : 35 min
★ Very easy   ☆ Cheap

CARROT HALWA

1 kg finely grated carrot
400 gm sugar
150 gm unsalted butter
or ghee
100 gm ground almonds
3 soup sp flaked almonds
1 coffee sp elaichi (cardamom)
powder
20 gm ground almonds
3 litres milk

6 servings

Mix together the carrots and the milk, then place in a pan and bring to the boil. Simmer gently until the mixture is reduced by half. Add the sugar and continue cooking, stirring constantly.

Cook for a further 20 minutes on a low heat. Add the butter and the almonds and cook for 25 minutes in a moderate oven. The mixture should now be thick and coming away from the sides.

Remove from the oven and add the powdered elaichi. Stir in to mix well.

Turn the mixture out onto a buttered plate sprinkled with the ground almonds.

Allow to cook and cut into the traditional lozenge shapes.

Preparation : 15 min • Cooking : 1 h
★ Easy   ☆ Cheap

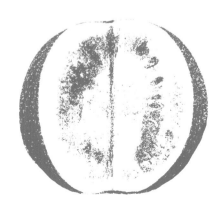

ORANGE CARAMEL CREAM

150 gm sugar
60 ml water
2 oranges for the juice and zest
2 egg yolks
5 large eggs
120 ml fresh cream
2 tots Grand Marnier
½ litre milk

5 servings

Place 100 gm of the sugar in a clean pan and cover with just sufficient water. Stir to dissolve. Place on a fierce heat and bring to the boil.

When the sugar begins to turn a light caramel colour, remove from the heat, add the orange zest and juice.

Place the pan in a bowl of cold water to stop further cooking. Be careful here as the water bubbles with the heat from the pan. Warm the milk in a pan to blood heat.

Beat the egg yolks, cream, grand marnier, 50 gm of sugar and the milk together and strain.

Pre-heat the oven to 250°F (140°C). Pour a little of the caramel into 5 separate dishes. Allow to set a little.

Pour the egg custard mix into individual dishes. Place the dishes into a larger casserole. Pour the water up to ½ the height of the dishes. This prevents the custard from becoming too hot and boiling.

Turn the oven down to 200°F (120°C). Place into the oven and allow to cook.

When the egg custard is set, remove from the oven and allow to cool.

Turn out from the dish and serve either hot or cold.

Preparation : 10 min • Cooking : 30 min
★ Easy   ☆ Cheap

ELAICHI FLAN

½ litre fresh milk
4 medium whole eggs
1 egg yolk
¼ coffee sp elaichi (cardamom) powder
60 gm sugar

5 servings

Pre-heat the oven to 200°F (120°C).

Warm the milk, whisk the eggs, yolk, elaichi and the sugar together. Pour in the warm milk and whisk together. Strain through a fine strainer and pour into 5 moulds. Place the moulds into a baking dish. Pour water into the dish until the level is ⅔ of the way up the moulds. Place gently in the oven.

Cook until firm, about 20 minutes, then remove from the oven.

Serve hot or cold.

Preparation : 5 min • Cooking 25 min
★ Very easy   ☆ Cheap

SYRUP BASE FOR SORBETS

1 litre water
650 gm sugar
200 gm glucose

Dissolve all the ingredients in a clean bowl then place in a very clean pan and bring to the boil.

Remove carefully any scum that may surface.

When boiled for 2 minutes, remove from the heat.

Preparation : 5 min • Cooking : 3 min
★ Very easy   ☆ Cheap

SORBET OF CHINESE GUAVA

¾ litre Chinese guava pulp
½ litre sorbet base syrup
1 lemon squeezed for the juice

6 servings

Strain the pulp from the seeds.
Add the rest of the ingredients together.
Place into a sorbetier and process or into a bowl in the deep freeze and whisk well every 5 minutes until of a smooth frozen consistency.
Serve with a little of the guava syrup and just a taste of kirsch.

Preparation : 15 min
★ Easy   ☆ Cheap

MANGO SORBET

1 litre sorbet base syrup
1 lemon squeezed for the juice
¾ litre mango pulp

6 servings

Mix all the ingredients together.
Place into a sorbetier and process, or into a bowl in the deep freeze and whisk well every 5 minutes until of a smooth frozen consistency.
Serve with a little of the mango syrup with just a taste of Drambuie.

Preparation : 15 min
★ Very easy   ☆ Cheap

AVOCADO SORBET

½ litre sorbet base syrup
2 lemons squeezed for the juice
½ litre avocado pulp

6 servings

Mix all of the ingredients together. Work quickly before avocado browns.
Place into a sorbetier or a bowl in the deep freeze and whisk well every 5 minutes until of a smooth frozen consistency.

Preparation : 15 min
★ Easy   ☆ Cheap

BLACKCURRANT SORBET

½ litre sorbet base syrup
1 lemon squeezed for the juice
¾ litre blackcurrant pulp

6 servings

Strain the pulp from the seeds and combine with the rest of the ingredients.
Place into a sorbetier and process, or into a bowl in the deep freeze and whisk well every 5 minutes until of a smooth frozen consistency.
Serve with a little of the blackcurrant syrup with just a taste of white rum.

Preparation : 15 min
★ Very easy   ☆ Cheap

Right: Wild Raspberries for Davinia (p. 152)
Right page: Clockwise from top: Blackcurrant Sorbet, Mango Sorbet, Sorbet of Chinese Guava, Avocado Sorbet

COCONUT BREAD

620 gm plain sieved flour
2¼ tsp baking powder
¼ tsp ground cloves
450 gm castor sugar
1 pinch salt
200 gm freshly grated coconut
60 gm butter (melted)
357 ml milk

makes 3 loaves

Pre-heat oven to 300°F (160°C).

Grease and flour 3 small bread tins.

Mix all the dry ingredients together well with a wooden spoon. Pour in a quarter of the milk and stir well. Continue with the milk, pouring a quarter at a time, blending well after each addition. Stir in the melted butter.

Fill the bread tins with the mixture, not more than ⅔ full and bake the bread for approx. 1 hour.

Remove from the oven and allow to cool for about 5 minutes in a tin.

After 5 minutes turn the bread out on to a wire rack.

Serve warm or cool.

Note: If dessicated coconut is used, steep it in milk for half an hour before draining well, then proceed as above.

Preparation : 15 min • Cooking : 1 h
★ Very easy　　☆ Cheap

COCONUT BARS

750 gm unsalted butter
180 gm brown sugar
300 gm plain flour
625 gm brown sugar
4 beaten eggs
1 tsp baking powder
120 gm freshly shredded coconut
2 drops vanilla essence
1 level tsp salt

200 × 2.5 cm square

Preheat the oven to 350°F (180°C).

Blend together the butter, the 180 gm sugar and 300 gm flour.

Press into the base of a well-greased 15 cm square pan and prick with a fork.

Cook in oven until a light brown then remove.

Beat the rest of the ingredients together and spread over the baked crust. Bake again for 15 minutes.

Cut into 2.5 cm squares when cool.

Note: Dessicated coconut may be used in the place of the fresh, although it is always best to use fresh whenever possible.

Preparation : 20 min • Cooking : 30 min
★ Easy　　☆ Cheap

TROPICAL GINGER MOUSSE

4 leaves gelatine or 10 gm powdered
140 ml milk
2 egg yolks
40 gm sugar
50 gm diced preserved ginger
10 ml ginger syrup
1 tot dark rum
2 egg whites
10 gm sugar for the egg whites
180 ml double cream, whipped

4 servings

Soak the gelatine leaves in cold water.
Bring the milk to the boil in a pan.
Remove from the heat.
Whisk together the egg yolks and the sugar until creamy. Slowly whisk in the hot milk.
Pour the liquid back into the saucepan and onto the heat.
Cook, stirring constantly until the mixture begins to thicken. Remove the pan from the heat.
Squeeze out the water from the gelatine leaves.
Whisk into the now thickened custard.
If necessary pass the custard through a sieve, place on ice to cool.
Add 25 gm of the diced preserved ginger. Add the ginger syrup and the rum and whisk well.
Whisk the egg whites until they stand in snowy peaks. Whisk in the 10 gm of sugar.
Fold in the whipped cream with a wooden spoon, into the cooled custard mixture.
Now fold in the whisked egg whites very gently.
Spoon the mousse into 4 glasses and allow to set in a refrigerator.
Sprinkle on top the remaining diced ginger.

Preparation : 10 min
★ Easy ☆ Moderate

COCONUT WATER JELLY

30 gm agar agar or 20 gm of gelatine
1 litre fresh coconut water
small scoops fresh tender coconut flesh
sugar to taste

4 servings

Melt the agar agar or gelatine in 50 ml of warm water. Add the coconut water and cook for 15 minutes on a low heat. Add the sugar to your own taste.
Pour into small serving dishes and add the coconut flesh. Place into the refrigerator to set.
Serve well chilled.

Preparation : 10 min • Cooking : 15 min
★ Very easy ☆ Cheap

BANANAS WITH COCONUT FLAMBE

12 large bananas
125 gm unsalted butter
125 ml caramel sauce
4 oranges for the zest and squeezed for the juice
3 lemons for zest and squeezed for the juice
¼ tsp cinnamon powder
1 freshly grated coconut (dessicated)
4 tots dark rum, warmed
1 tsp honey

6 servings

Peel the bananas and cut into half.
Heat the butter in a pan and cook the bananas gently for about 5 minutes. Pour in the caramel sauce. Add the fruit juice, zest, cinnamon, honey and the coconut. Cook for a further 2 minutes.
Pour over the warm rum and light.
Serve immediately.

Preparation : 10 min • Cooking : 7 min
★ Very easy ☆ Cheap

COCONUT MOUSSE

½ litre milk
100 gm freshly grated fine coconut or
dessicated coconut
15 gm gelatine (or 12 leaves)
5 egg yolks
75 gm castor sugar
3 egg whites
190 gm castor sugar
water for boiling sugar
5 gm cornflour

6 servings

Bring the milk and the coconut to the boil. Soften the gelatine in some cold water.

Whisk the yolks and 75 gm of the sugar together. Add the cornflour and whisk well.

Pour the hot milk onto the egg yolk mixture. Simmer for a few minutes on a low heat and allow to cool.

Whisk the egg whites with 95 gm sugar. If you are using gelatine leaves, remove them from the water and melt them gently.

Boil 95 gm of sugar with some water to 120°F. If you have no thermometer cook until sugar forms a soft ball when drop-

ped into cold water — about 15 minutes. Add this to the whisked egg whites and whisk well. Add the melted gelatine and again whisk well. Allow the merigue to cool. Fold the thickened cream mixture into the meringue very gently. Pour the mixture into moulds and refrigerate for 2 hours.

Preparation : 15 min • Cooking : 10 min
★ Difficult   ☆ Cheap

Bottom left: Coconut Mousse
Bottom right: Coconut Pancake

COCONUT PANCAKE

For pancake:
120 gm milk
70 gm plain flour
1 egg yolk
1 large whole egg
30 gm sugar
45 gm melted butter

For filling:
120 gm freshly flaked coconut
2 tots coconut liqueur (Coco Rico)
25 ml caramel sauce

4 servings

Mix together the milk and the flour thoroughly. Add the yolk egg and the sugar, mix well.

Add 15 gm of the melted butter and whisk well, then pass the mixture through a very fine sieve.

Mix the coconut; coconut liqueur and caramel together with the rest of butter, keep this mixture aside.

Fry very thin pancakes. Fill the pancakes with the coconut mixture. Cover with a butter paper and keep warm in the oven. Sprinkle with castor sugar just before serving.

Preparation : 15 min • Cooking : 10 min
★ Very easy   ☆ Cheap

WILD RASPBERRIES FOR DAVINIA

40 gm sugar
15 gm marzipan
1 small egg
35 gm plain flour
1 pinch cinnamon
8 tblsp fresh cream
300 ml smooth raspberry puree
8 balls vanilla ice cream
500 gm raspberries marinated
in Grand Marnier
(Strawberries are also delicious)

8 servings

Cream together the sugar, marzipan, and the egg. Do not whisk to a froth.

Sieve the flour, cinnamon and the salt together and stir into the creamed egg mixture. Pass through a sieve and allow to stand for 1 hour.

Stir in one dessert spoon of fresh cream.

Grease a baking sheet and dust lightly with flour. Spread out the mixture evenly to a circle, 10 cm in diameter.

Bake in a 180°F (100°C) oven for 3–4 minutes. Slide the baking sheet half way out of the oven to ensure that the biscuits do not get cold and unworkable.

Lift the discs off the tray with a palette knife. Drop them over a cup and press gently with a cloth to form the shape. One must work very quickly as the disc will crispen in 1 minute.

Pour the raspberry puree onto the plate. Mark the puree with a 'spider' of fresh cream.

Place the biscuit onto the puree, then place a ball of ice cream into the biscuit, then cover the ice cream with the raspberries.

Serve immediately.

Preparation : 20 min. • Cooking : 4 min
★ Difficult   ☆ Moderate

PUMPKIN GATEAU

800 gm pumpkin flesh
150 gm sugar
150 gm plain flour
120 gm unsalted butter
oil for deep frying
extra sugar

15 gâteaux

Cut the pumpkin flesh into pieces and steam until soft. Mash until smooth with a fork; when this is done place in a bowl add the rest of the ingredients and beat very well until a smooth paste. Roll into flat round pieces.

Heat the oil in a pan until very hot.

Fry the gateau until a golden brown. Scoop out onto a wire rack to drain. Sprinkle with extra sugar and serve warm.

Note: Try and use pumpkin with red flesh as it is sweeter.

Preparation : 20 min • Cooking : 10 min
★ Very easy   ☆ Cheap

CHINESE NEW YEAR CAKE

225 gm soft brown sugar
700 gm glutinous rice powder
225 ml boiling water

1 cake

Prepare a Chinese steamer by lining with clear cellophane.

Mix the sugar and the water together. Stir until the sugar is totally dissolved. Add the glutinous rice and mix well into a paste. Pour the rice paste into the lined steamer, and put steamer over a high heat. Allow to steam for 2 hours.

When cooked, remove from the steamer and allow to cool. Let the cake stand for two days before eating.

Note: Cover the outside of the steamer with a damp cloth to retain steam.

Preparation : 10 min • Cooking : 2 h
★ Difficult   ☆ Cheap

LYCHEE DUMPLING

1 kg large potatoes
250 gm unsalted butter softened
to working consistency
100 gm semolina
20 gm salt
1 egg
2 egg yolk
200 gm plain flour
5 gm baking powder
200 gm brioche crumbs
20 lychees peeled

20 dumplings

Wash the potatoes under running cold water. Bake the potatoes in a very hot oven.

When totally cooked; remove the potatoes from the oven.

Allow to rest for 20 minutes. Whilst still warm, cut the potatoes in half. Remove the flesh from the skin with a spoon.

Mash with a fork until totally smooth.

Make a well in the middle of the potato.

Into the well, add 100 gm of the softened butter, the semolina, salt, egg and the egg yolks.

Sieve the flour and the baking powder together, and add to the potato.

Mix together and knead well to form a smooth dough.

If necessary more flour may be added.

Cover and refrigerate for approximately 15 minutes.

Remove the paste from the refrigerator and roll out 5 mm thick on a floured board.

Cut into squares and wrap a lychee into each square. Roll it into a ball in the palm of your hands.

Continue until 20 dumplings are made.

Bring 2 litres of water to the boil. Place the dumplings in the water for about 15 minutes.

Scoop out of the water and refresh them under cold water.

Heat the remaining butter in a pan.

Fry the brioche crumbs until a golden brown, stirring all the time.

Roll the dumplings into the golden crumbs.

Serve warm, dusted with icing sugar.

Preparation : 25 min • Cooking : 20 min
★ Easy   ☆ Moderate

PEANUT BISCUITS

125 gm smooth peanut butter
80 gm unsalted butter
15 gm honey
180 gm sugar
1 large egg
1 yolk
150 gm plain flour sieved
5 gm salt
60 gm crushed peanuts

Pre-heat oven to 180°F (100°C).

Cream the peanut butter, butter, honey and the sugar together. Beat together very well.

Add the egg and the yolk. Beat in well.

Add the sieved flour and salt to the above mixture slowly. Beat well all the time.

Roll out the pastry to the desired thickness. Cut into shapes and place onto a baking sheet.

Sprinkle with the crushed peanuts and press them into the dough a little.

Cook for 10 minutes in the oven. Remove from the oven and allow to cool.

Best eaten the same day.

Preparation : 10 min • Cooking : 10 min
★ Very easy   ☆ Cheap

TEMPTING
TODDIES

"Ho-Ho-Ho and a bottle of rum", wrote Robert Louis Stevenson in *Treasure Island* and the famous pirates' expression was born. I am sure that our Surcouf and his fellow marauders did not take long to persuade the Mauritians of former times that sugar cane was not only useful for producing sugar but also for distilling rum, a favourite drink in many of the world's tropical island states.

About four hectares of sugar cane will produce some 300 gallons of rum. As Mauritius is literally swamped by sugar cane, rum production is a major occupation; some of it is of the throat-burning type, and this is still illicitly distilled and consumed in the more remote villages, despite strict police surveillance.

In every town and in most villages you will find small, gaily-painted bars that dispense the island's elixir to a population thirsty from a day's toil under the tropical sun. The average Mauritian family will, however, have its own distinctive home-prepared variety flavoured with dry raisins, orange or lime peels, a stick or two of vanilla — all a closely-guarded secret. Mauritius has concentrated traditionally on the production of colourless and "green" rums, sporting varying degrees of alcoholic content and mainly made for local consumption.

Soon made aware, however, of the popularity of lighter and drier varieties, such as Bacardi, in the USA and UK, the island gave birth to a classic-to-be in *Green Island Rum*. Rivalling any light dry rum, *Green Island* is attractively bottled and makes an excellent base for many cocktails, blending perfectly with the several exotic ingredients that go into their making.

Darker and more mature rums, often aged in oak casks, which can sometimes be charred to enhance the flavour and colouring, are used in famous island punches. The abundance of tropical fruits in Mauritius, from passion fruit to pineapple, sometimes combined with coconut water, milk or cream, are excellent additives to the rum base.

In Mauritius, cocktails and punches are not just a matter of mixing or shaking the ingredients and serving them in a glass. They provide the artistic bartender with a golden opportunity to excel in the lavish use of fresh coconuts, pineapples and papayas as containers and of tropical flowers as decoration. The finished product thus looks too good to drink and very often inspires the tourists to go winging back to their rooms for their cameras!

PINEAPPLE ROYAL

2 tots dark rum
½ tot fresh lime juice
1 orange squeezed for the juice
60 ml fresh pineapple juice
10 ml sugar syrup
crushed ice

Place all of the ingredients into a blender for 1 minute.
Pour into a glass and serve.

Preparation : 10 min
★ Very Easy   ☆ Expensive

SAINT GERAN SUN PASSION

1 tot white rum
1 tot Coco Rico
75 ml coconut milk
75 ml strained fresh pineapple juice
15 ml fresh lime juice
1 pinch cinnamon powder
60 ml sugar syrup (30 gm sugar to 20 ml
water boiled until sugar is dissolved)
crushed ice

Place all of the ingredients into a blender. Blend on top speed and pour into a tall glass.

Preparation : 3 min
★ Very easy   ☆ Moderate

SUN EXCELLENCE

1½ tots white rum
1 tot Coco Rico
½ champagne glass fresh passion fruit juice or pineapple juice
1 scoop vanilla ice cream
1 dash Grenadine syrup

Blend all of the ingredients together.
Pour in a champagne flute half full with crushed ice; add a dash of Grenadine syrup.

Preparation : 5 min
★ Very easy   ☆ Moderate

ISLAND PUNCH

2 tots white rum
½ tot orange curacao
1 tot fresh lime juice
1 orange squeezed for the juice
30 ml fresh pineapple juice
20 ml grenadine
crushed ice

Place all of the ingredients into a shaker.
Shake very well and pour into a glass.

Preparation : 5 min
★ Very Easy   ☆ Expensive

THE CORAL REEF

1 tot cherry brandy
1 tot creme de cacao (brown)
1 dash fresh lime juice
60 ml fresh coconut milk
1 orange squeezed for the juice
crushed ice

Shake all of the items together well. And pour into a glass.

Preparation : 10 min
★ Very Easy   ☆ Expensive

PAUL AND VIRGINIE PUNCH

crushed ice
½ tot Grenadine syrup
1½ tots Praline Grille liqueur
1½ tots dark rum
½ glass fresh orange juice
½ glass fresh strained pineapple juice

Place crushed ice into a long glass. Pour the Grenadine syrup around the glass.
Shake the rest of the ingredients well. Pour over the crushed ice.

Preparation : 5 min
★ Very easy   ☆ Moderate

LYCHEE PUNCH

1½ tots white rum
1½ tots Coco Rico
½ wine glass fresh
or canned lychee juice
1 ball vanilla ice cream
crushed ice

Place all the ingredients into a blender. Blend for 30 seconds on top speed.
Pour into a wine glass and serve.
Decoration of the glass: Dip the top rim of the glass into a little egg white then dip straight into a tray of coloured sugar to line the rim.

Note: For fresh lychee juice, remove the brown outside skin and the stone leaving only the flesh of the lychee.
Place this flesh into a blender with a little water to puree.
Strain gently through a fine strainer.
This makes an excellent cooler if drunk very cold.

Preparation : 5 min
★ Very easy   ☆ Moderate

SUN DREAM

1 banana
juice of 1 fresh lemon
½ glass fresh strained pineapple juice
1 tot Praline Grillee liqueur
1½ tots dark rum
1 dash Grenadine

Blend the banana, lemon juice and pineapple juice first.
Then add the liqueurs, shake for 10 seconds. Pour into a long glass half full with crushed ice.
Add a dash of Grenadine.
Decoration: A slice of orange, 2 cherries on a thin wooden skewer and a red hibiscus flower.

Preparation : 5 min
★ Very easy   ☆ Moderate

BANANA PUNCH

1 fresh banana
juice of 1 fresh lemon
1 tot banana liqueur
2 tots white rum
crushed ice

Blend the banana with the lemon juice. Add the rest of the ingredients, blend for 30 seconds.
Pour into a wine glass.

Preparation : 15 min
Very Easy • Cheap

COCO DE LUXE

2 tots white rum
1 tot brandy
½ tot fresh lime juice
1 orange squeezed for the juice
60 ml fresh pineapple juice
60 ml fresh coconut milk
20 ml grenadine
crushed ice

Place all the ingredients together in a shaker.
Shake well and pour into a glass.

Preparation : 10 min
★ Very Easy   ☆ Expensive

MAURITIAN PEARL

1 tot Gordon's gin
1 tot green chartreuse
2 tots Rose's lime juice
juice of 1 lemon

Shake all of the ingredients and pour over crushed ice into a tulip glass.
Decoration: A slice of lemon, a cherry and flowers.

Preparation : 5 min
★ Very easy   ☆ Moderate

HALLEY'S COMET COCKTAIL

2 mangoes
2 tots dark rum
1 tot Van der Hum liqueur
1 lemon squeezed for juice
½ glass fresh strained pineapple juice
½ tsp. honey

Peel and cut the flesh from the mango.
Blend all ingredients for 30 seconds except the crushed ice.
Pour over crushed ice in a tall glass.

Preparation : 10 min
★ Very easy   ☆ Moderate

Left: Sun Dream
Middle: Dodo Cocktail
Right: Creole Punch

CREOLE PUNCH

2½ tots white rum
2 fresh limes, squeezed
½ tot sugar cane syrup
crushed ice

Decoration of the wine glass: Dip the rim of the glass into egg white then dip into sugar.
Cocktail: Place all ingredients into a shaker, except the ice. Shake well and pour into a glass over the crushed ice.

Preparation : 5 min
★ Very easy   ☆ Moderate

COFFEE AND COCO PUNCH

2 tots coconut liqueur
1 ball chocolate ice cream
cold black coffee
25 ml fresh double cream
crushed ice
roasted coconut

Place all the ingredients into a blender except the coconut. Blend for 30 seconds.
Pour into a chilled wine glass. Sprinkle the roasted coconut on top.

Preparation : 5 min
★ Very easy   ☆ Moderate

SAINT GERAN COOLER

crushed ice
½ glass ginger ale
½ tot Cointreau
½ tots white rum
1 lemon squeezed for juice
½ tot Grenadine

Place the ice in a long glass.
Shake the rest of the ingredients well except for the Grenadine. Pour the shaken ingredients over the ice and add the Grenadine.

Preparation : 5 min
★ Very easy   ☆ Moderate

DODO COCKTAIL

150 ml fresh pineapple juice
2 tots white rum
1 tot cherry liqueur
dash Grenadine
crushed ice

Strain the fresh pineapple juice.
Pour all of the ingredients into a blender. Blend on top speed and pour into a balloon glass.

Preparation: 2 min
★ Very easy   ☆ Moderate

159

GLOSSARY

Achards : This word is derived from the Persian *atchar* and describes various fruits or vegetables which are pickled and highly spiced. Very popular in India and the Mascarene islands.

Ajinomoto : Also known as monosodium glutamate (MSG) — a vegetable salt which is often used in oriental cooking as a flavouring agent.

Allspice : A West Indian spice belonging to the noble family of Myrtaceae. Allspice gives off a strong aroma, somewhere between cloves, nutmeg and cinnamon, and therefore should be used sparingly.

Anise : The anise plant is found all over the Mediterranean as well as in the northern regions of Europe. Its leaves resemble those of parsley and in this form it may be used to liven up the taste of certain root vegetables. The seed of the green anise is used in sweet and savoury cooking.

Bamboo : A giant reed which grows in India and other hot countries. The young shoots are widely used in the Far East. In India they are pickled with vinegar and peppery spices and called *achards*.

Banana leaves : Preference is given to pale young leaves. Used as a fragrant wrapper for fish, meat, or vegetables, in either roasting or steaming. Aluminium foil may be used as a substitute.

Basil : Is best used when fresh when is at its most fragrant and flavoursome.

Bay leaves : More commonly used dry and as an ingredient of the "bouquet garni" which is a frequently used flavouring agent for soups, stews and sauces.

Bilimbie : A bitter fruit grown in Mauritius. Two different types are grown; the round bilimbie is grape size; the long bilimbie grows to a length of 5 cm.

Caraway : A seed which is blackish, narrow and curved like a crescent moon. The taste is less peppery than cumin and the aroma is similar to anise.

Cardamom : Cardamom is a vital ingredient in curries, forming the basic flavour of *garam massala*. Available in two forms, black or green. The black seeds come in large pods, which contain clusters of seeds and are used as an important curry spice in garam masala and also as fragrant spice in sweets. The smaller greenish pods have a mild lemon fragrance and are also used as a sweet or savoury spice. Can also be bought in powder form.

Chatini : A local synonym for chutney.

Chinese Mushrooms : Dried black mushrooms which need to be soaked in warm water for 20 minutes. Japanese shiitake are similar in appearance, but have a totally different flavour.

Chutney : An accompaniment to many Mauritian dishes. Basically composed of a purée of fruits or vegetables mixed with spices and vinegar. Most popular are mango, tamarind, tomato, coconut and aubergine.

Cinnamon : The bark of an exotic laurel plant, originally from Sri Lanka. Used to flavour both sweet and savoury dishes. Cassia is similar to cinammon but has a much coarser flavour.

Citronelle : Known elsewhere as Vervain, is a lemon-scented plant that is used in Mauritius as an infusion instead of tea.

Cloves : A spice from the clove tree grown particularly in Malagasy, Zanzibar and Indonesia. Introduced into Mauritius by Governor Poivre, a minister of Louis XV. Only a small amount should be used in cooking.

Coriander : Dried coriander seeds give off an aroma of both anise and pepper which becomes more pronounced once it is roasted. The leaves, known in Mauritius as "Chinese parsley", lose their rather strong aroma in cooking.

Court – Bouillon : An aromatic and spiced infusion in which fish or shell-fish are cooked for a short period.

Cumin : Used in the preparation of curries, the cumin seed is yellowish, oblong and ribbed, slightly larger than the anise seed.

Curry : One of the most well known of all the oriental spice mixtures. Everyone claims to have the "real" curry powder. Our recipe for curry powder is found on page 117.

Curry leaves : A fragrant leaf which is a vital ingredient of Mauritian curries, known locally as *carri poulé.*

Dholl : The local name for yellow split peas, used extensively in Mauritian cuisine. There are many recipes featuring this nutritious food throughout the book.

Fenugreek : Used in Indian cuisine, where the dried seeds are crushed into powder (for curries and chutney, etc). The fresh leaves are often used as a vegetable in India. Dried seeds smell of burnt sugar and have a slightly bitter taste.

Fruits de cythie : A Mauritian fruit used when it is green and bitter, for *achards* and chutneys.

Garam masala : A blend of spices prepared as a curry paste or as a condiment for Indian cooking. Unlike curry powder does not contain chilli powder or turmeric. Keeps for up to one month in an airtight container.

Ginger : Often used in fresh root form in Mauritius where it is readily available. Has a very peppery, distinctive taste which can be a pleasant addition to both fish and meat.

Ghee : Clarified butter which is the main cooking medium in Indian cuisine.

Julienne : Finely shredded vegetables or meat.

Lentils : Dried black beans which, together with dholl (see above), are used as vegetables or accompaniments to many Mauritian dishes.

Mange tout : A sugar pea of which the pod is eaten as well as the seeds.

Manioc : Also known as *cassava*, used whole as a root vegetable or ground into flour and used as a substitute for wheat flour.

Marjoram : This aromatic herb is used in cookery from the flower labiate.

Mazavarro : A Mexican condiment made of ground red peppers preserved in oil.

Natural Yoghurt : Used extensively in Indian cooking to enrich the food.

Okra : Known in Mauritius as *lalo* or ladies' fingers. Can be used as a vegetable or in the making of Gumbo soups.

Peanut : Known as *pistache de terre* (groundnuts) in Mauritius because the shells drag on the ground when the moment of ripeness is reached. Used in a wide variety of recipes.

Rice : Basmati and Patna are the best known types of long grain rice.

Rosemary : The leaves of this evergreen are used extensively for seasoning, fresh or dried. The leaves are narrow, green and hard with a strong aromatic smell.

Saffron : This is the term used locally for turmeric. It should not be confused with the highly-priced Spanish saffron as often happens. It is, however, used for the same purpose — for colouring and seasoning rice.

Sesame : White sesame seeds are used as a garnishing or a flavouring agent and the oil is often used in Chinese cooking.

Soy sauce : Commonly found as a condiment on the dining tables of the Far East. An excellent salt substitute as well as flavouring agent.

Tamarind : The fruit of the tamarind tree is a 12 cm pod containing reddish pulp and small string of seeds. The pulp is highly acidic and has an unusual flavour. Used in condiments, chutneys, *achards* and *rougailles*.

Turmeric : Known as saffron in Mauritius. It is a very hot yellow powder and gives the characteristic yellow tinge to curries or rice.

Vanilla : The pod of the vanilla plant grown in Mauritius is odourless when fresh: however it exudes an agreeable aroma when added to sugar or boiled in milk. It is an indispensable ingredient in Creole punches.

INDEX

164

ACKNOWLEDGEMENTS

For their help in making this book, the authors and the publisher would
like to thank the following people: Lynda Cunden, Paquerette Leung
Chack Hing, Geneviève Hervet, Mesh Boyjonauth and Mr Kalooa
Vijranand, the "brigade" of the Saint Geran Sun Hotel, Jacqueline and
Clothilde Dalais, Brigitte Eynaud, Deven Chinapiel, Régis Fanchette,
O.B.E., Sun International Hotels, Ghislaine Supparayen, Mr & Mrs
Maurice Chu, MacMillan Publishing Company, Air Mauritius, Rodney
Phillips, Mrs Peerally, Mrs L. Rountree and Polaroid – Singapore.

Photographs of the dishes were taken by Gerald Gay at the Touessrock,
Saint Geran and La Pirogue Hotels, with the kind collaboration of
Sun International.

Foreword by **Michel Rostang**
Texts and recipes by **Barry Andrews** and **Paul Jones**
Photographs by **Gerald Gay** except
p 8 (top) by **Michel Folco**; pp 4–5, 9 (bottom),
11 (top), 12 (bottom), 15 (bottom) by **Rosine Mazin**